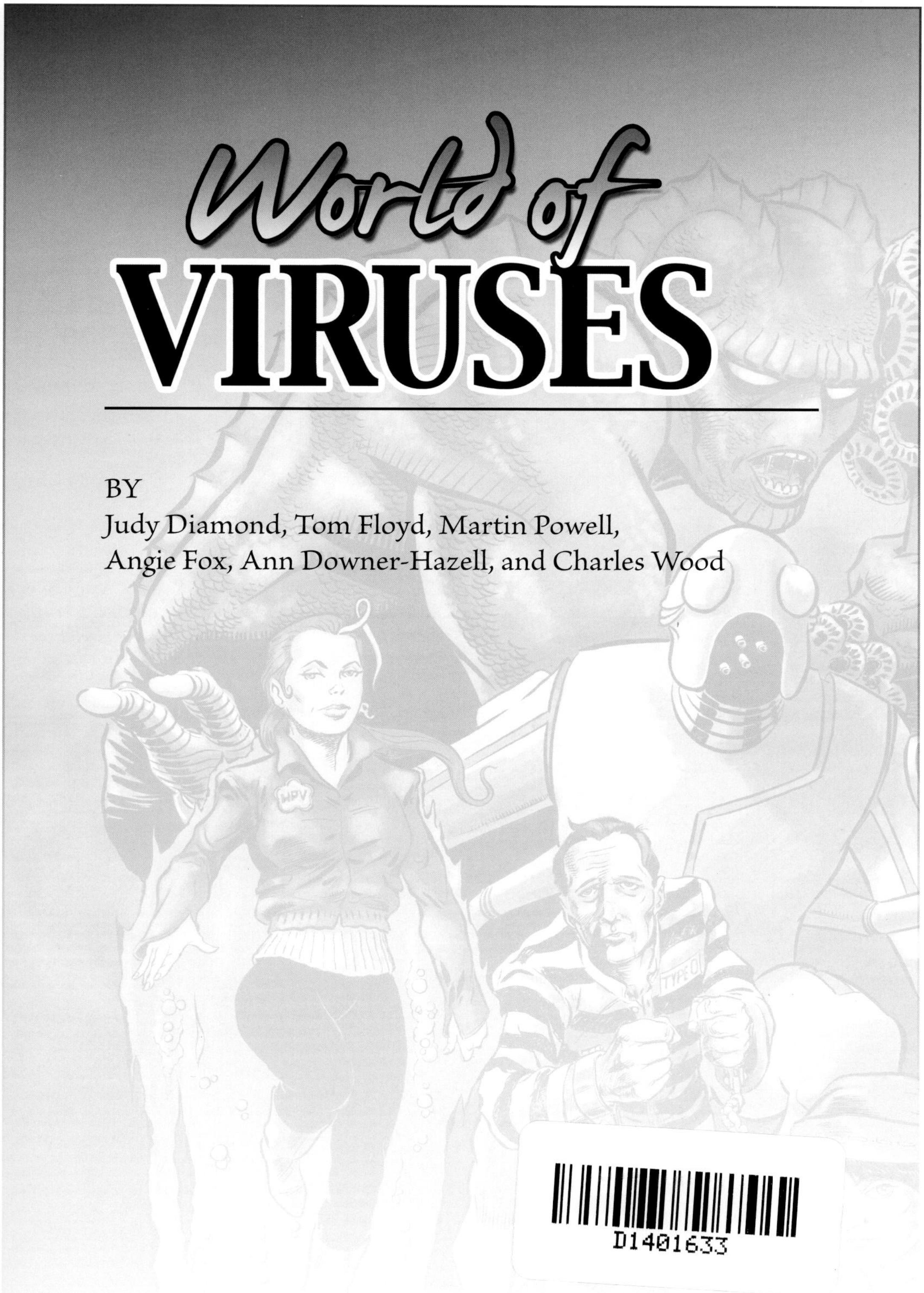

World of VIRUSES

BY
Judy Diamond, Tom Floyd, Martin Powell,
Angie Fox, Ann Downer-Hazell, and Charles Wood

UNIVERSITY OF NEBRASKA PRESS • LINCOLN & LONDON

Cataloging-in-Publication Data on file with the Library of Congress.

World of **VIRUSES** is an alliance of science educators, media professionals, and virology researchers working to increase public understanding about viruses and infectious disease. For information see www.worldofviruses.unl.edu. This book is a collaboration of scientists, educators, and artists, made possible by the creative efforts of the following illustrators and writers:

Art by **TOM FLOYD**
The Curse of the Tree-Man inks by **JOSEF RUBINSTEIN** & colors by **SCOTT BEACHLER**
The Never-Ending Battle art by **BRENT SCHOONOVER**
Stories by **MARTIN POWELL**
Scientific illustration & production by **ANGIE FOX**
Essays by **ANN DOWNER-HAZELL**
Science Director, **CHARLES WOOD**
Project Director, **JUDY DIAMOND**

This project was supported by the National Center for Research Resources and the Division of Program Coordination, Planning, and Strategic Initiatives of the National Institutes of Health through Grant Number R25 RR024267. Its content is solely the responsibility of the authors and does not necessarily represent the official views of NCRR or NIH.

SEPA SCIENCE EDUCATION PARTNERSHIP AWARD
Supported by the National Center for Research Resources, a part of the National Institutes of Health

University of Nebraska Lincoln

THE NEBRASKA CENTER FOR VIROLOGY
A Partnership of the University of Nebraska-Lincoln, the University of Nebraska Medical Center, and Creighton University Medical Center.
http://www.unl.edu/virologycenter

SOUNDPRINT MEDIA CENTER, INC.

SOUNDPRINT MEDIA CENTER, INC.
Radio stories ranging from the hard investigative to the evocative experiential documentary. Real-life science behind the comics – hear the stories of survivors, researchers, and scientists who overcome obstacles to solve the mysteries of the World of Viruses.
http://soundprint.org

University of Nebraska State Museum

THE UNIVERSITY OF NEBRASKA STATE MUSEUM
Explore Nebraska's natural science heritage.
http://www.museum.unl.edu

Contents

FOREWORD by Carl Zimmer   p. 1

INTRODUCTION   p. 3

FOOT AND MOUTH DISEASE VIRUS
    CONFINED! Graphic Story   p. 6
    TERROR ON THE FARM Essay   p. 17

HUMAN IMMUNODEFICIENCY VIRUS
    PHANTOM PLANET Graphic Story   p. 20
    DOOMSDAY VIRUS Essay   p. 31

EMILIANIA HUXLEYI VIRUS
    NEVER–ENDING BATTLE Graphic Story   p. 34
    DEADLY BLOOM Essay   p. 45

INFLUENZA VIRUS
    FROZEN HORROR Graphic Story   p. 48
    WAKING THE DEAD Essay   p. 59

HUMAN PAPILLOMAVIRUS
    CURSE OF THE TREE-MAN Graphic Story   p. 61
    CURSED! Essay   p. 79

Foreword

By Carl Zimmer

Drawing dividing lines through nature can be scientifically useful, but when it comes to understanding life itself, those lines can end up being artificial barriers. Rather than trying to figure out how viruses are not like other living things, it may be more useful to think about how viruses and other organisms form a continuum. We humans are an inextricable blend of mammal and virus. Remove our virus-derived genes, and we would be unable to reproduce. We would probably also quickly fall victim to infections from other viruses. Some of the oxygen we breathe is produced through a mingling of viruses and bacteria in the oceans. That mixture is not a fixed combination, but an ever-changing flux. The oceans are a living matrix of genes, shuttling among hosts and viruses.

Drawing a bright line between life and nonlife can also make it harder to understand how life began in the first place. Scientists are still trying to work out the origin of life, but one thing is clear: it did not start suddenly with the flick of a great cosmic power switch. It's likely that life emerged gradually, as raw ingredients like sugar and phosphate combined in increasingly complex reactions on the early Earth. It's possible, for example, that single-stranded molecules of RNA gradually grew and acquired the ability to make copies of themselves. Trying to find a moment in time when such RNA-life abruptly became "alive" just distracts us from the gradual transition to life as we know it.

Banning viruses from the Life Club also deprives us of some of the most important clues to how life began. One of the great discoveries about viruses has been the tremendous diversity in their genes. Every time scientists find new viruses, most of their genes bear little resemblance to any gene ever found before. The genes of viruses are not a meager collection of DNA cast off in recent years from true living things. Many scientists now argue that viruses contain a genetic archive that's been circulating the planet for billions of years. When they try to trace the common ancestry of virus genes, they often work their way back to a time before the common ancestor of all cell-based life. Viruses may have first evolved before the first true cells even existed. At the time, life may have consisted of little more than brief coalitions of genes, which sometimes thrived and sometimes were undermined by genes that acted like parasites.

Patrick Forterre, a French virologist, has even proposed that in the RNA world, viruses invented the double-stranded DNA molecule as a way to protect their genes from attack. Eventually their hosts took over their DNA, which then took over the world. Life as we know it, in other words, may have needed viruses to get its start.

At long last, we may be returning to the original two-sided sense of the word *virus,* which originally signified a life-giving substance or a deadly venom. Viruses are indeed exquisitely deadly, but they have provided the world with some of its most important innovations. Creation and destruction join together once more.

CARL ZIMMER
A Planet of
Viruses

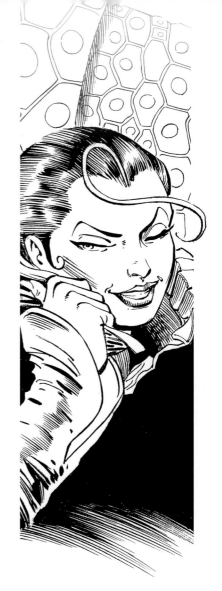

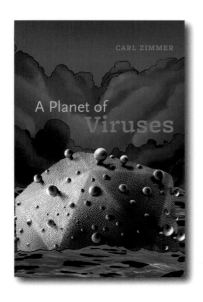

This foreword was excerpted with permission from Carl Zimmer's book, *A Planet of Viruses,* published by the University of Chicago Press in 2011. Carl Zimmer wrote the essays for *A Planet of Viruses* for the World of Viruses project. To purchase this book, see http://www.press.uchicago.edu.

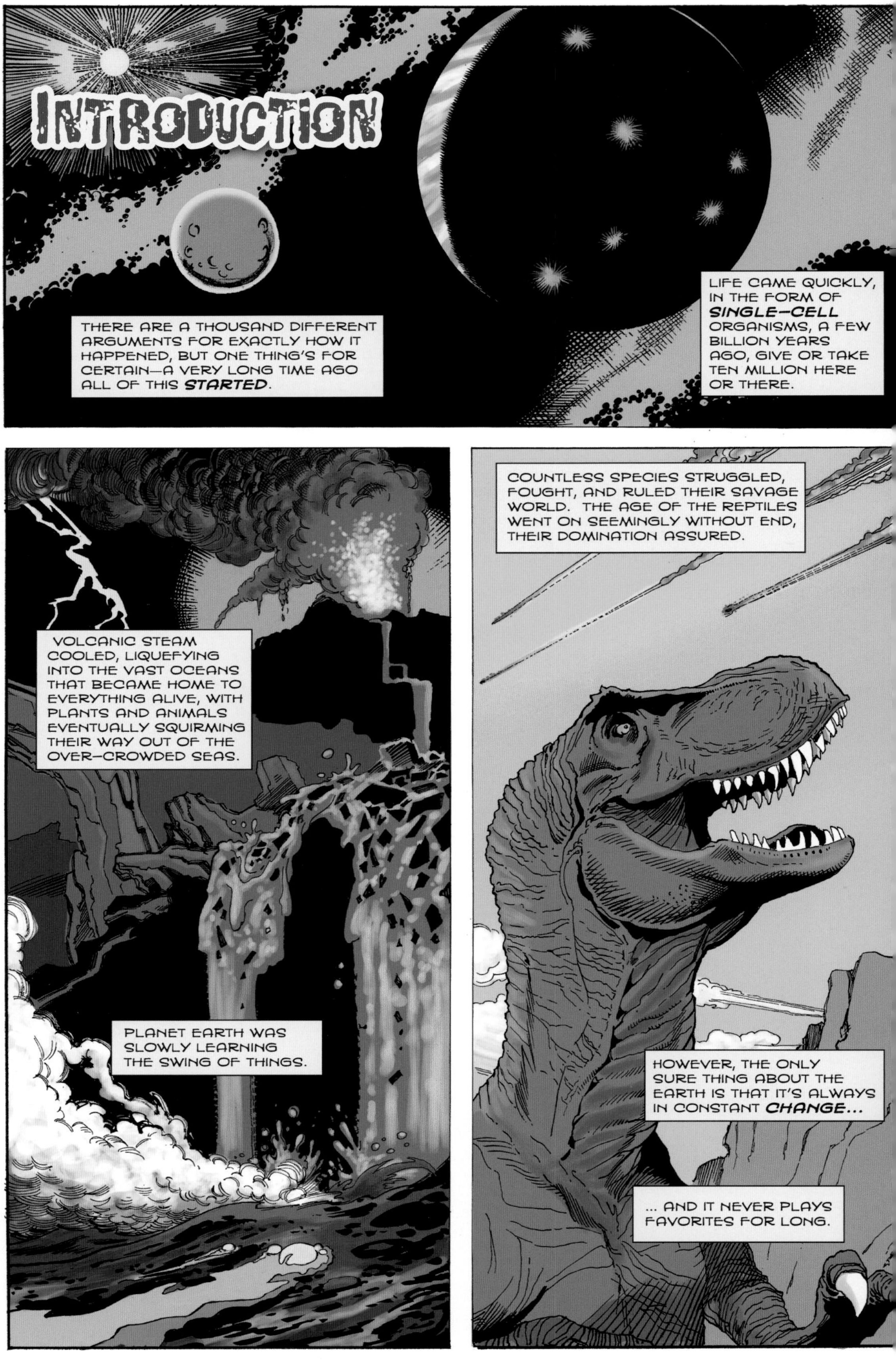
INTRODUCTION
THERE ARE A THOUSAND DIFFERENT ARGUMENTS FOR EXACTLY HOW IT HAPPENED, BUT ONE THING'S FOR CERTAIN—A VERY LONG TIME AGO ALL OF THIS STARTED.
LIFE CAME QUICKLY, IN THE FORM OF SINGLE-CELL ORGANISMS, A FEW BILLION YEARS AGO, GIVE OR TAKE TEN MILLION HERE OR THERE.
VOLCANIC STEAM COOLED, LIQUEFYING INTO THE VAST OCEANS THAT BECAME HOME TO EVERYTHING ALIVE, WITH PLANTS AND ANIMALS EVENTUALLY SQUIRMING THEIR WAY OUT OF THE OVER-CROWDED SEAS.
PLANET EARTH WAS SLOWLY LEARNING THE SWING OF THINGS.
COUNTLESS SPECIES STRUGGLED, FOUGHT, AND RULED THEIR SAVAGE WORLD. THE AGE OF THE REPTILES WENT ON SEEMINGLY WITHOUT END, THEIR DOMINATION ASSURED.
HOWEVER, THE ONLY SURE THING ABOUT THE EARTH IS THAT IT'S ALWAYS IN CONSTANT CHANGE...
... AND IT NEVER PLAYS FAVORITES FOR LONG.

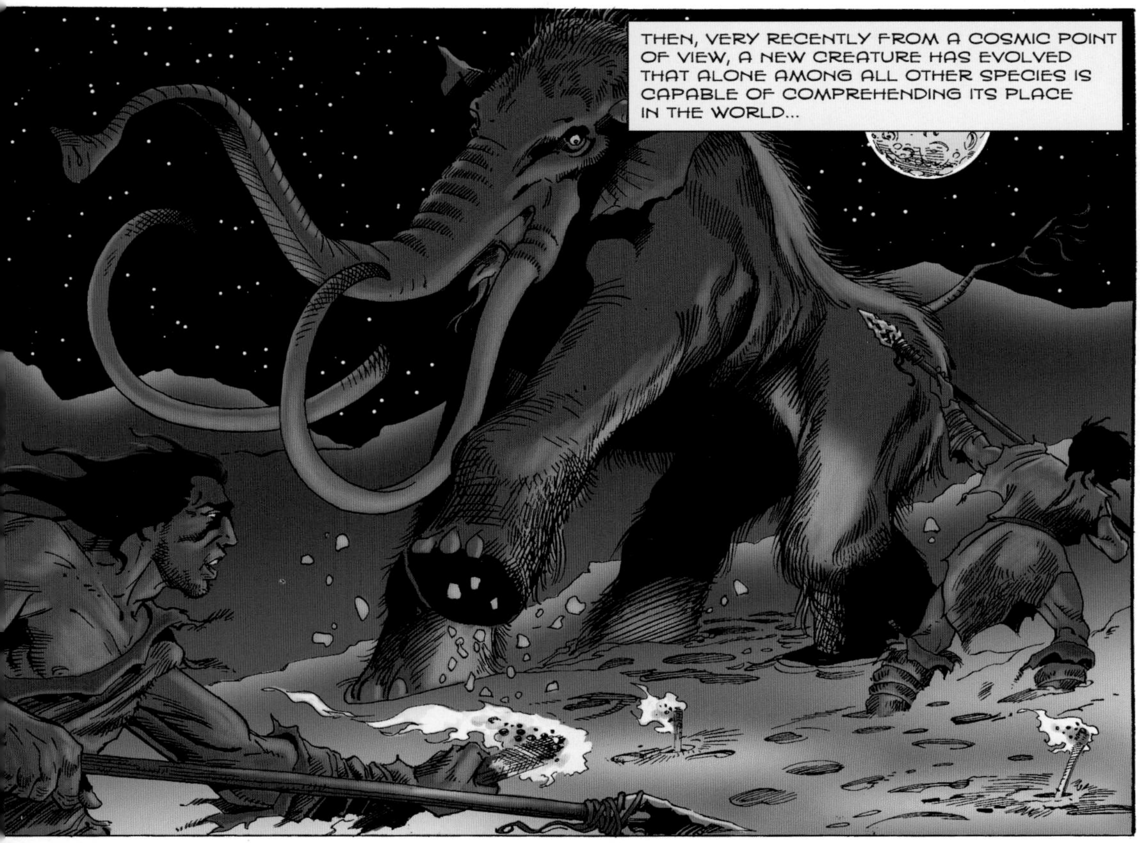
THEN, VERY RECENTLY FROM A COSMIC POINT OF VIEW, A NEW CREATURE HAS EVOLVED THAT ALONE AMONG ALL OTHER SPECIES IS CAPABLE OF COMPREHENDING ITS PLACE IN THE WORLD...

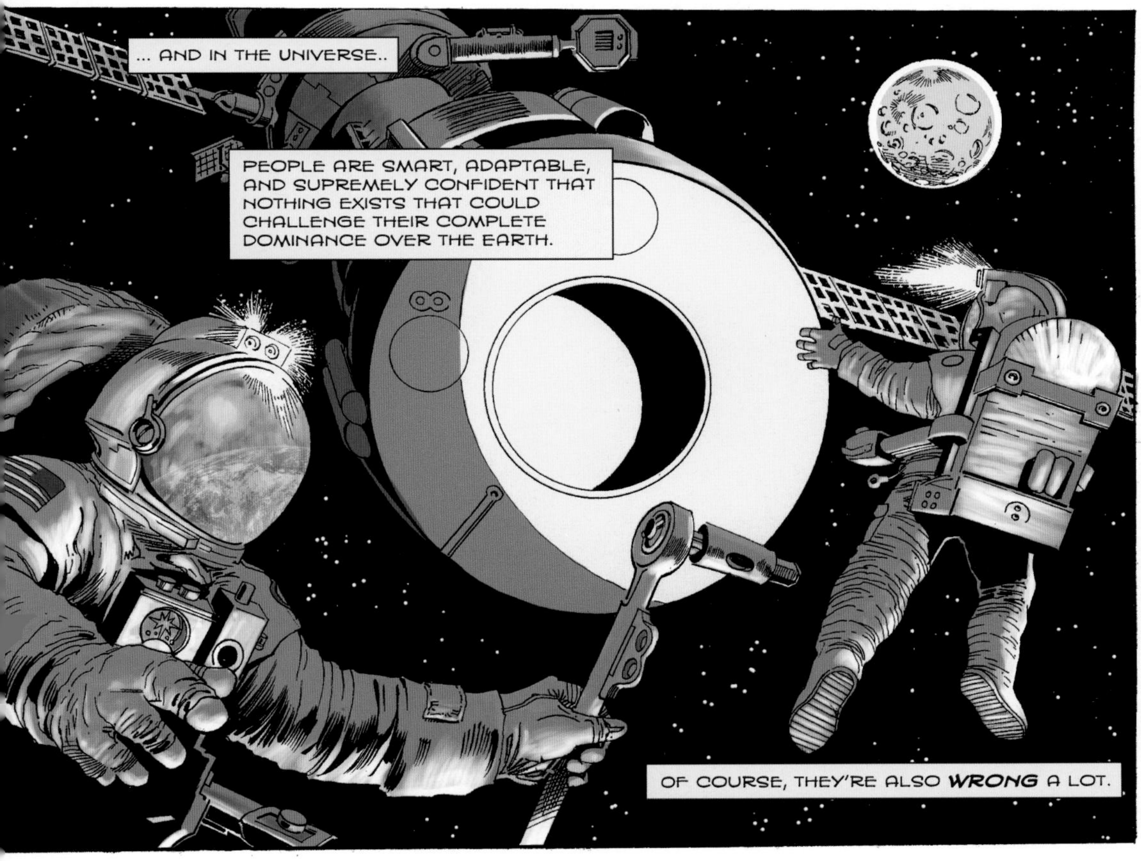
... AND IN THE UNIVERSE..
PEOPLE ARE SMART, ADAPTABLE, AND SUPREMELY CONFIDENT THAT NOTHING EXISTS THAT COULD CHALLENGE THEIR COMPLETE DOMINANCE OVER THE EARTH.
OF COURSE, THEY'RE ALSO ***WRONG*** A LOT.

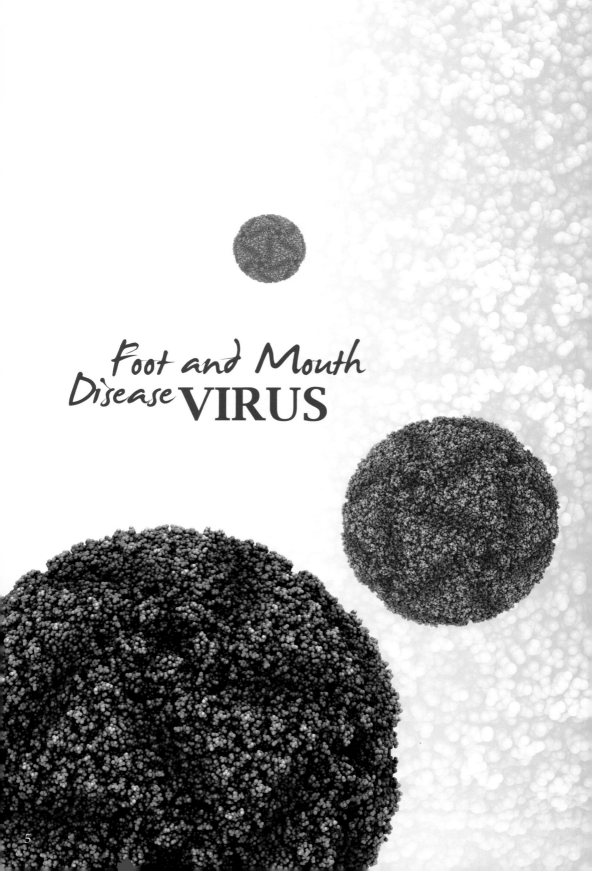

Foot and Mouth Disease VIRUS

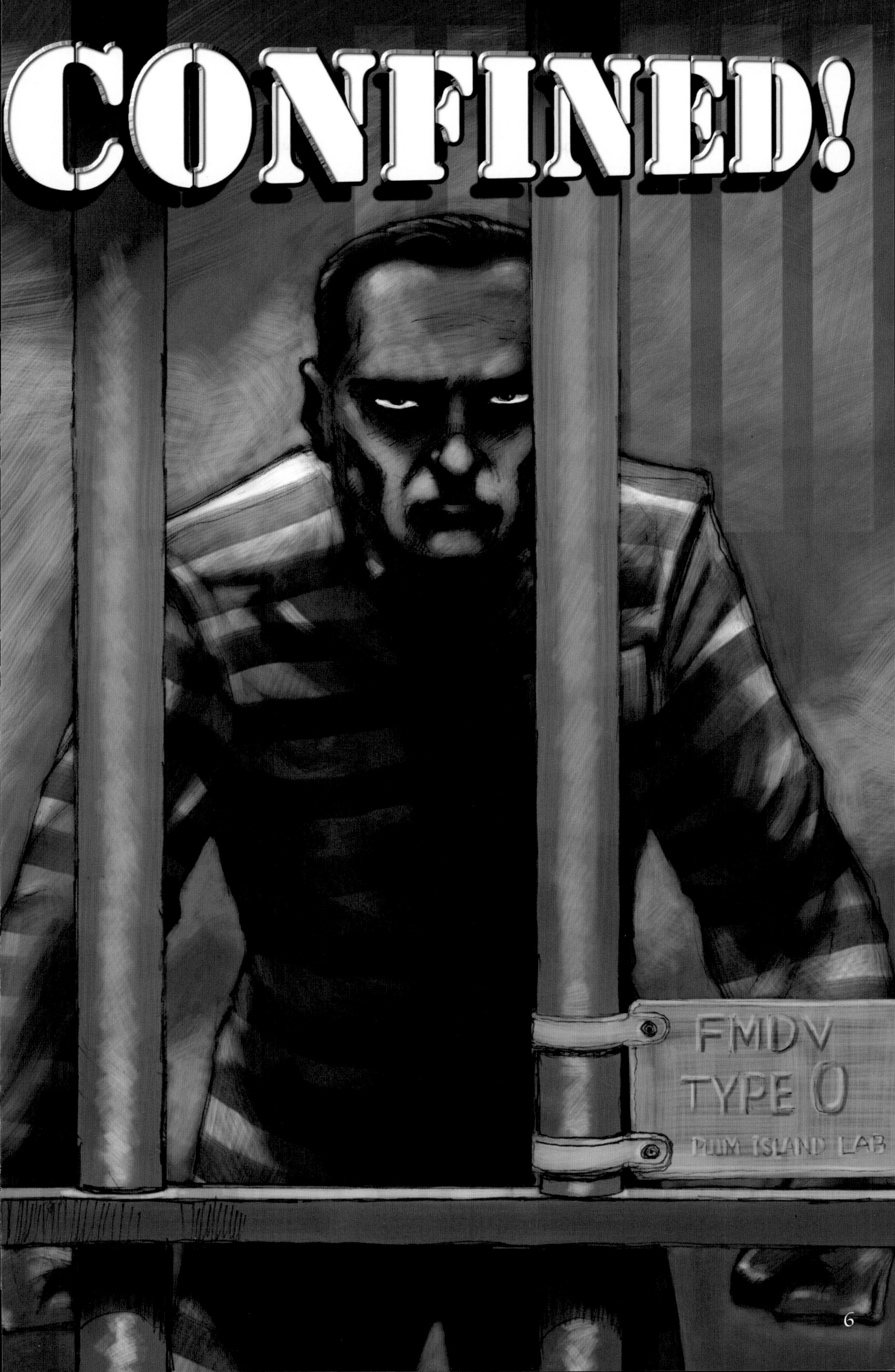
CONFINED!
FMDV
TYPE O
PLUM ISLAND LAB

CONFINED!

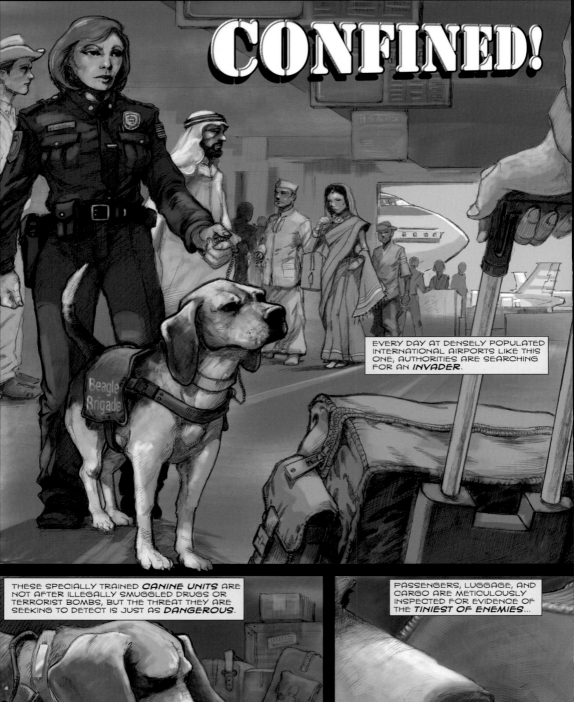

EVERY DAY AT DENSELY POPULATED INTERNATIONAL AIRPORTS LIKE THIS ONE, AUTHORITIES ARE SEARCHING FOR AN *INVADER*.

THESE SPECIALLY TRAINED *CANINE UNITS* ARE NOT AFTER ILLEGALLY SMUGGLED DRUGS OR TERRORIST BOMBS, BUT THE THREAT THEY ARE SEEKING TO DETECT IS JUST AS *DANGEROUS*.

PASSENGERS, LUGGAGE, AND CARGO ARE METICULOUSLY INSPECTED FOR EVIDENCE OF THE *TINIEST OF ENEMIES*...

...HIDDEN INSIDE A SEEMINGLY HARMLESS PIECE OF MEAT.

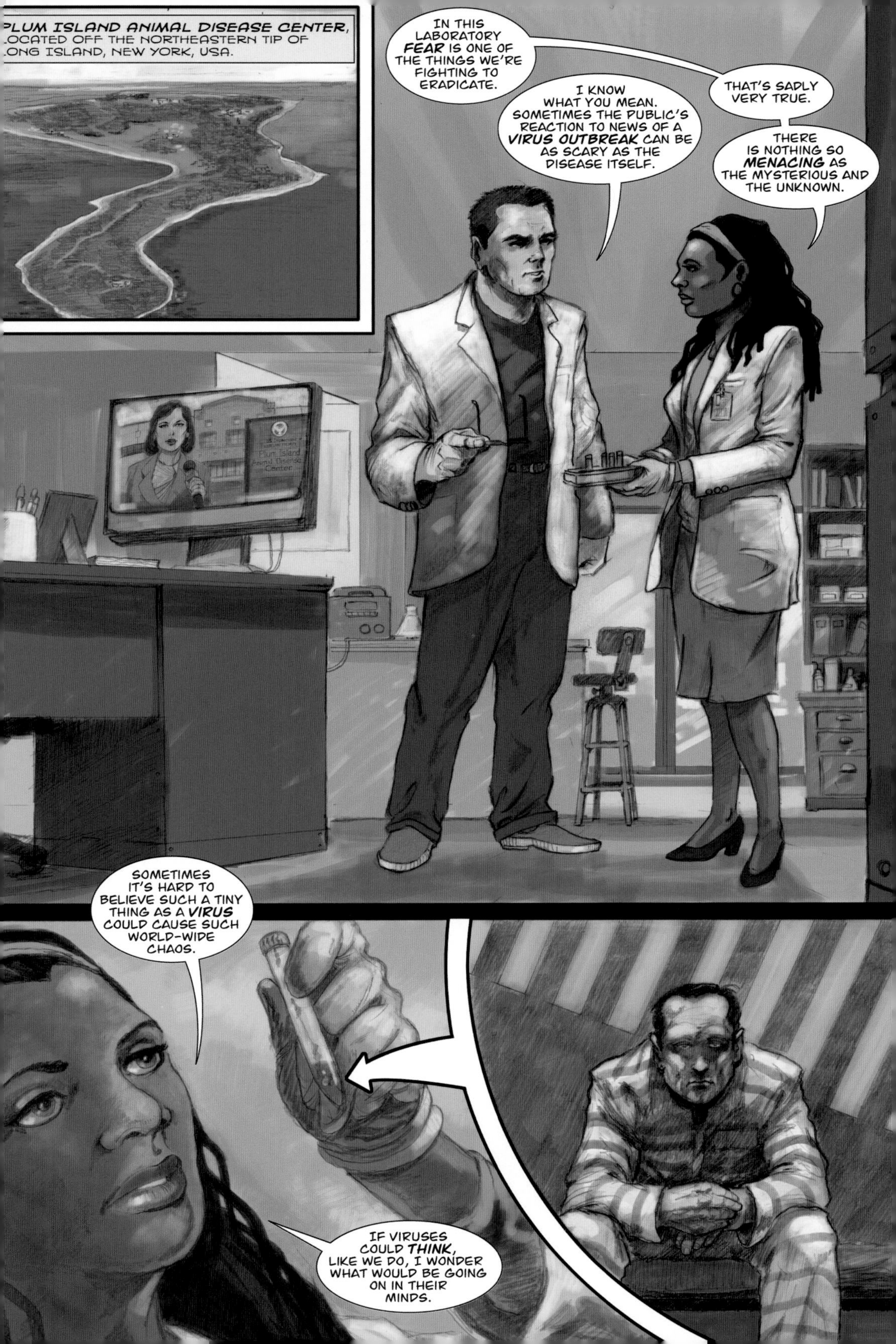
PLUM ISLAND ANIMAL DISEASE CENTER, LOCATED OFF THE NORTHEASTERN TIP OF LONG ISLAND, NEW YORK, USA.
IN THIS LABORATORY FEAR IS ONE OF THE THINGS WE'RE FIGHTING TO ERADICATE.
I KNOW WHAT YOU MEAN. SOMETIMES THE PUBLIC'S REACTION TO NEWS OF A VIRUS OUTBREAK CAN BE AS SCARY AS THE DISEASE ITSELF.
THAT'S SADLY VERY TRUE.
THERE IS NOTHING SO MENACING AS THE MYSTERIOUS AND THE UNKNOWN.
Plum Island Animal Disease Center
SOMETIMES IT'S HARD TO BELIEVE SUCH A TINY THING AS A VIRUS COULD CAUSE SUCH WORLD-WIDE CHAOS.
IF VIRUSES COULD THINK, LIKE WE DO, I WONDER WHAT WOULD BE GOING ON IN THEIR MINDS.

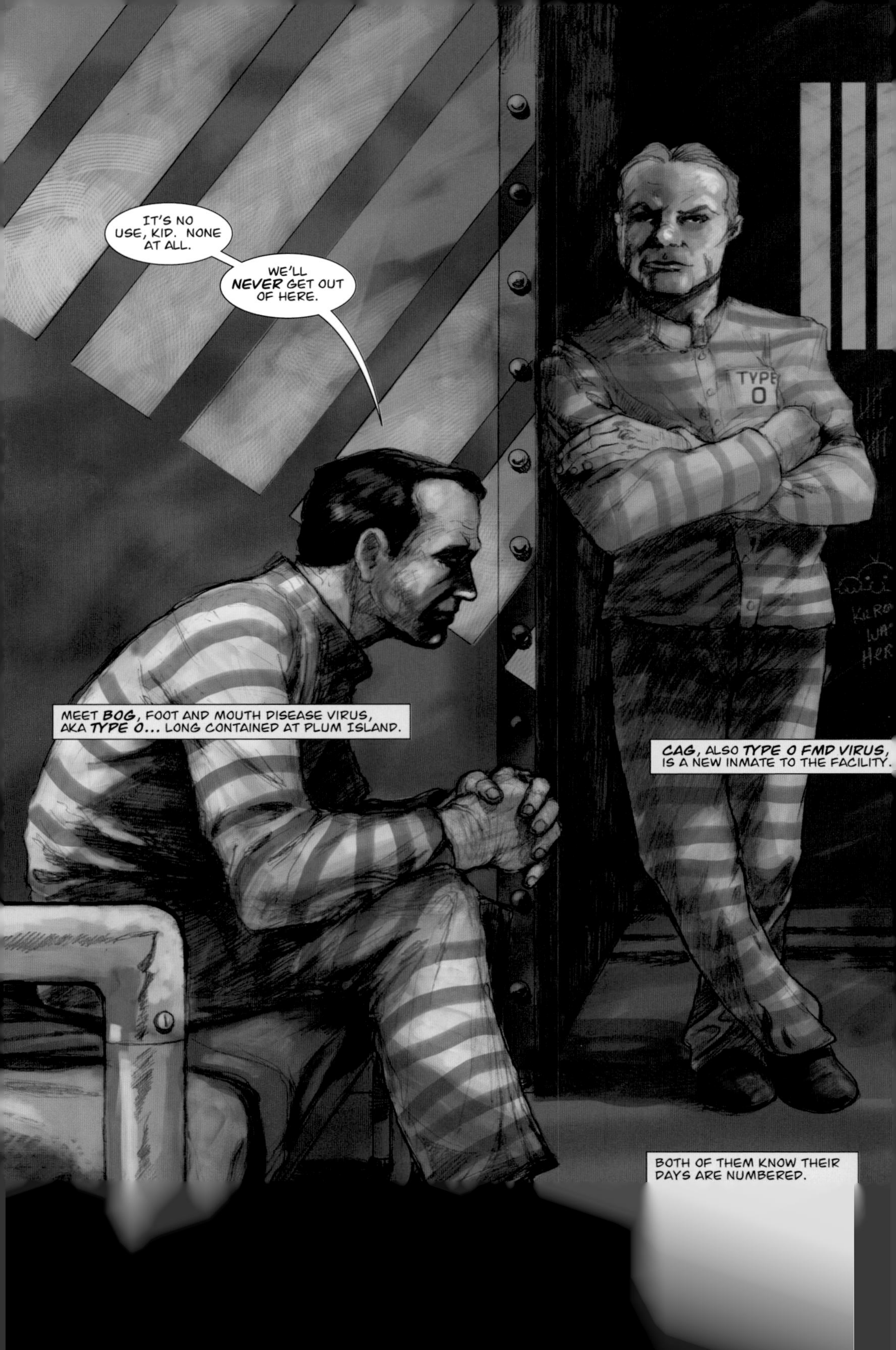
IT'S NO USE, KID. NONE AT ALL.
WE'LL NEVER GET OUT OF HERE.
MEET BOG, FOOT AND MOUTH DISEASE VIRUS, AKA TYPE O... LONG CONTAINED AT PLUM ISLAND.
TYPE O
CAG, ALSO TYPE O FMD VIRUS, IS A NEW INMATE TO THE FACILITY.
BOTH OF THEM KNOW THEIR DAYS ARE NUMBERED.

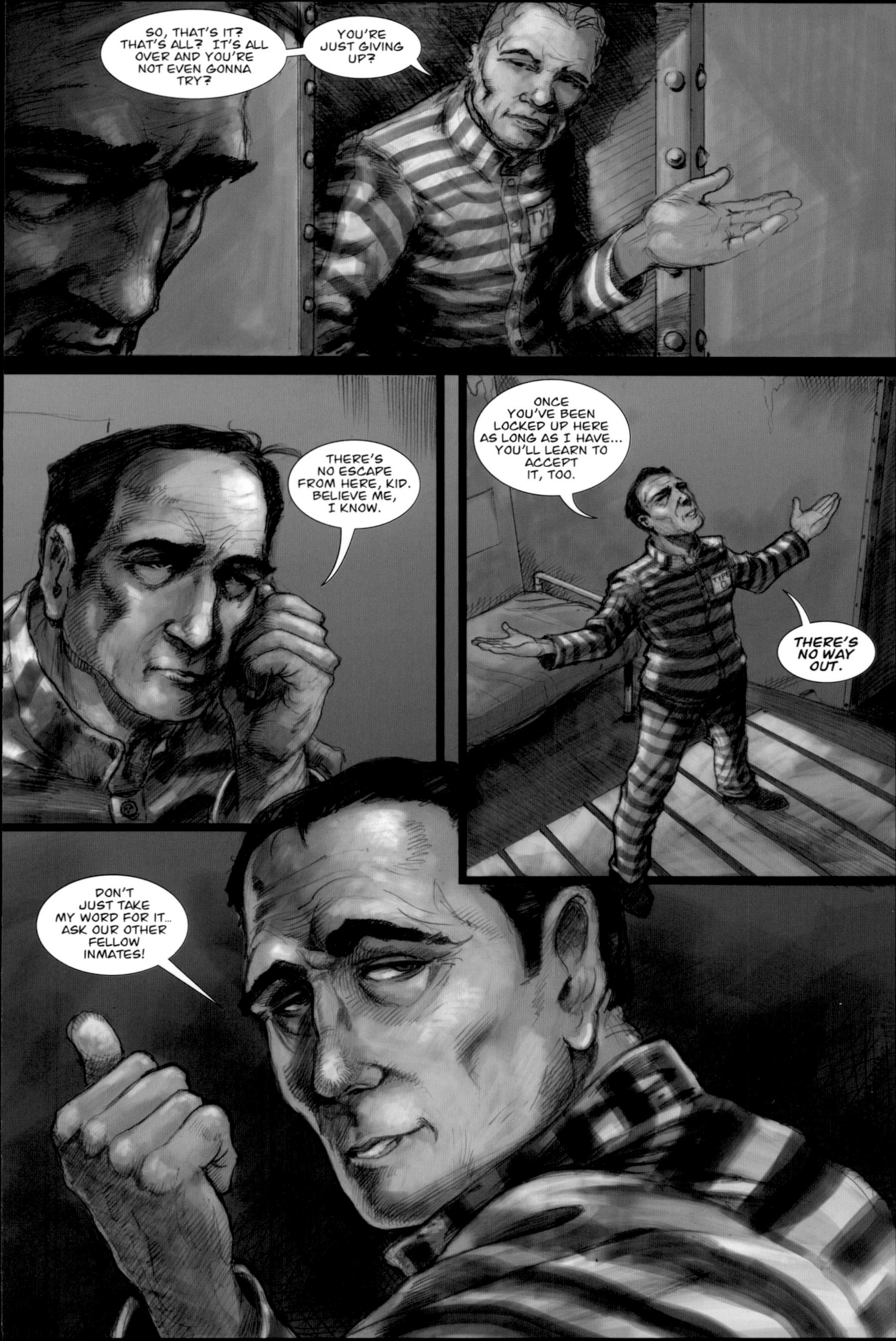
SO, THAT'S IT? THAT'S ALL? IT'S ALL OVER AND YOU'RE NOT EVEN GONNA TRY?
YOU'RE JUST GIVING UP?
THERE'S NO ESCAPE FROM HERE, KID. BELIEVE ME, I KNOW.
ONCE YOU'VE BEEN LOCKED UP HERE AS LONG AS I HAVE... YOU'LL LEARN TO ACCEPT IT, TOO.
THERE'S NO WAY OUT.
DON'T JUST TAKE MY WORD FOR IT... ASK OUR OTHER FELLOW INMATES!

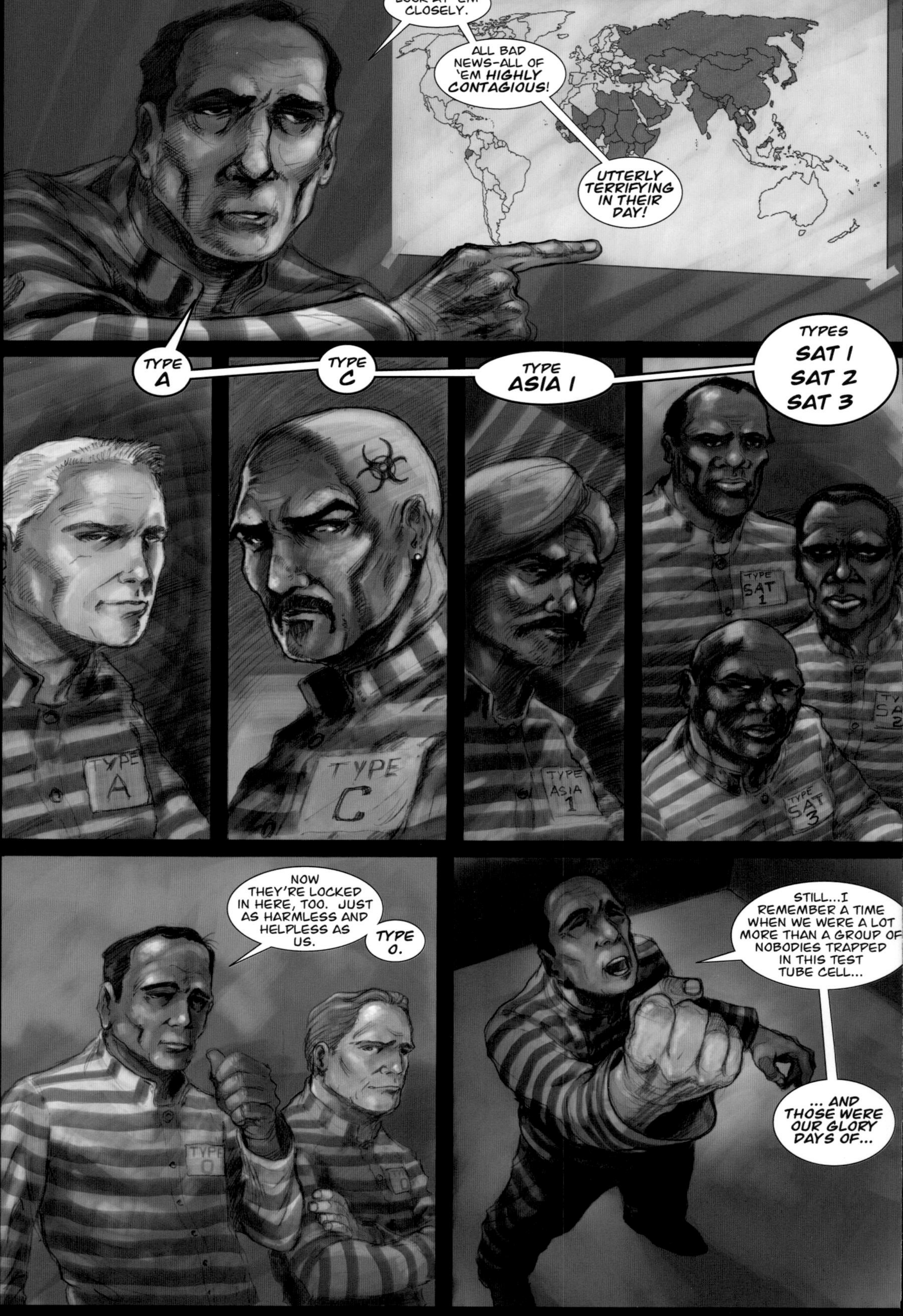
CLOSELY.
ALL BAD NEWS-ALL OF 'EM HIGHLY CONTAGIOUS!
UTTERLY TERRIFYING IN THEIR DAY!
TYPE A
TYPE C
TYPE ASIA 1
TYPES SAT 1 SAT 2 SAT 3
TYPE A
TYPE C
TYPE ASIA 1
TYPE SAT 1
TYPE SAT 3
NOW THEY'RE LOCKED IN HERE, TOO. JUST AS HARMLESS AND HELPLESS AS US.
TYPE O.
STILL...I REMEMBER A TIME WHEN WE WERE A LOT MORE THAN A GROUP OF NOBODIES TRAPPED IN THIS TEST TUBE CELL...
... AND THOSE WERE OUR GLORY DAYS OF...

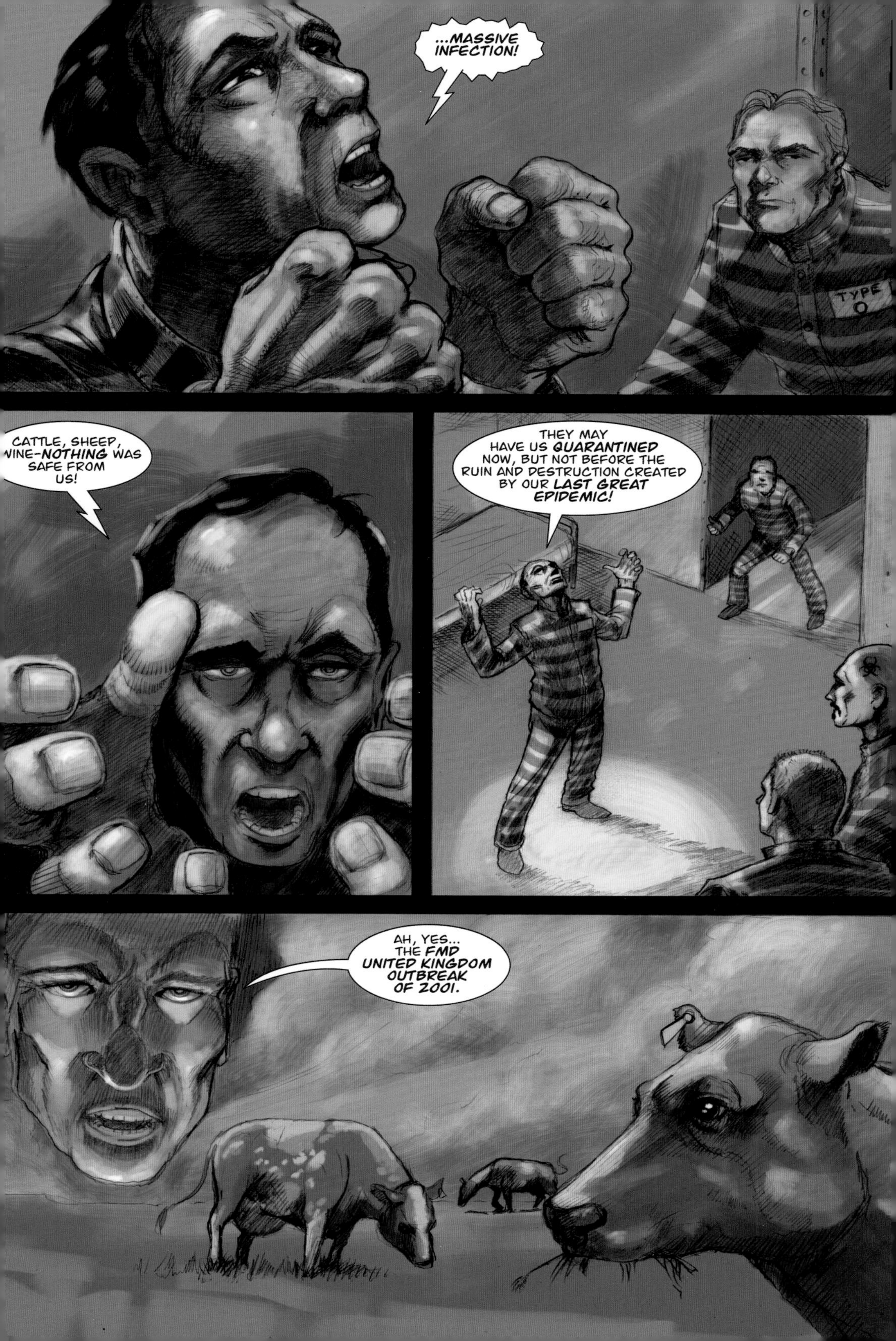
...MASSIVE INFECTION!
TYPE O
CATTLE, SHEEP, WINE-NOTHING WAS SAFE FROM US!
THEY MAY HAVE US QUARANTINED NOW, BUT NOT BEFORE THE RUIN AND DESTRUCTION CREATED BY OUR LAST GREAT EPIDEMIC!
AH, YES... THE FMD UNITED KINGDOM OUTBREAK OF 2001.

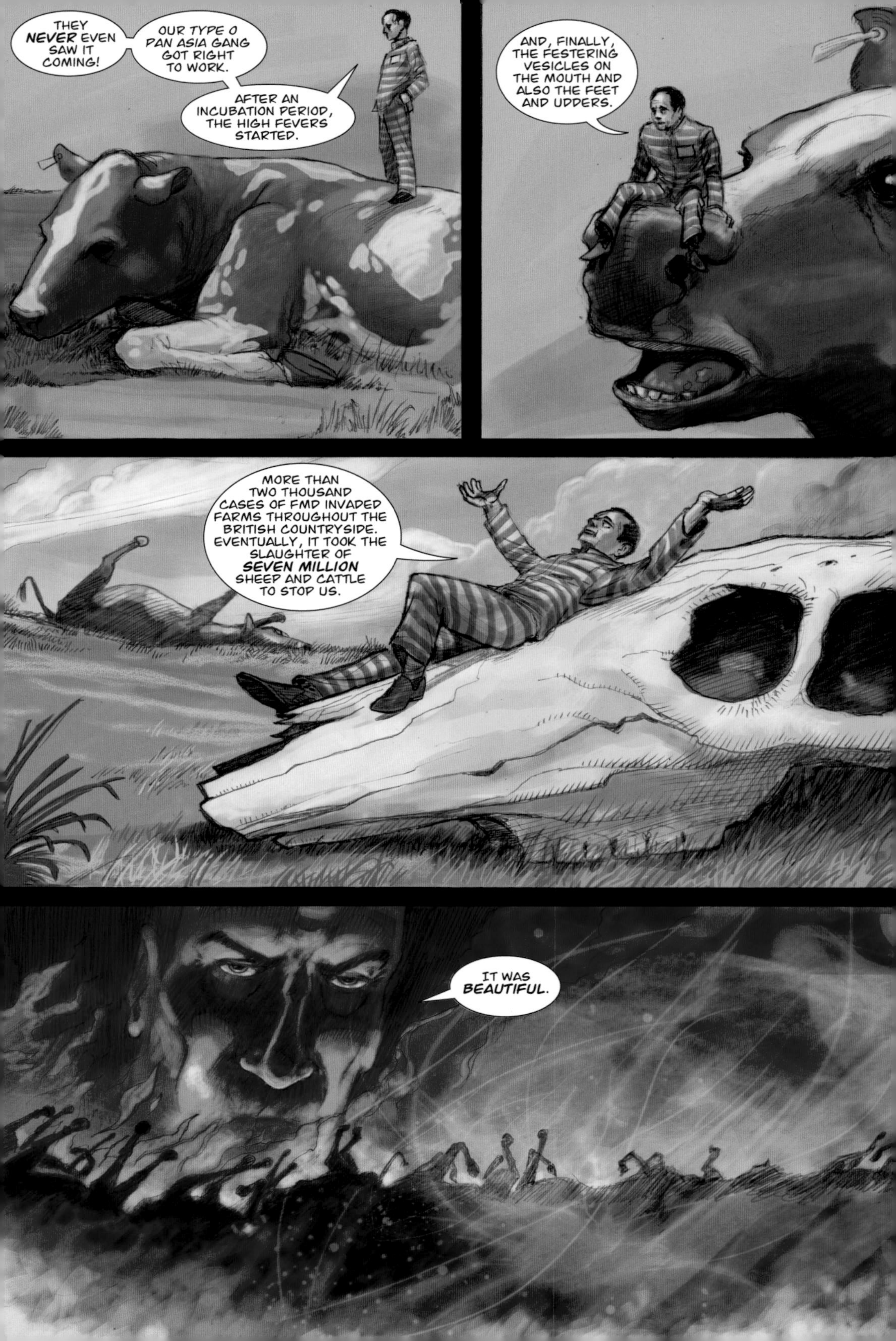
THEY **NEVER** EVEN SAW IT COMING!
OUR TYPE O PAN ASIA GANG GOT RIGHT TO WORK.
AFTER AN INCUBATION PERIOD, THE HIGH FEVERS STARTED.
AND, FINALLY, THE FESTERING VESICLES ON THE MOUTH AND ALSO THE FEET AND UDDERS.
MORE THAN TWO THOUSAND CASES OF FMD INVADED FARMS THROUGHOUT THE BRITISH COUNTRYSIDE. EVENTUALLY, IT TOOK THE SLAUGHTER OF **SEVEN MILLION** SHEEP AND CATTLE TO STOP US.
IT WAS **BEAUTIFUL**.

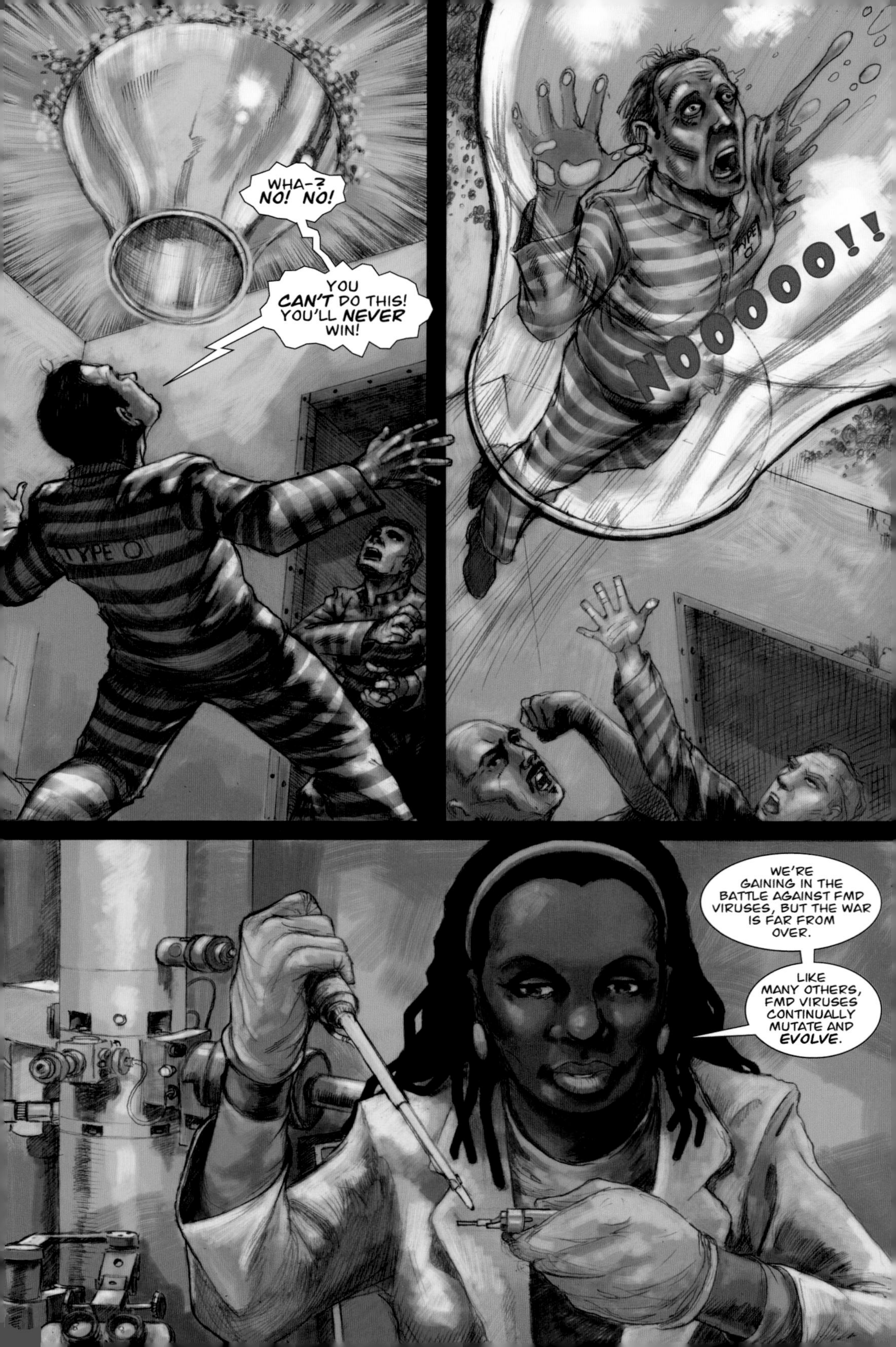
WHA-? NO! NO!
YOU CAN'T DO THIS! YOU'LL NEVER WIN!
TYPE O
NOOOOO!!
TYPE O
WE'RE GAINING IN THE BATTLE AGAINST FMD VIRUSES, BUT THE WAR IS FAR FROM OVER.
LIKE MANY OTHERS, FMD VIRUSES CONTINUALLY MUTATE AND EVOLVE.

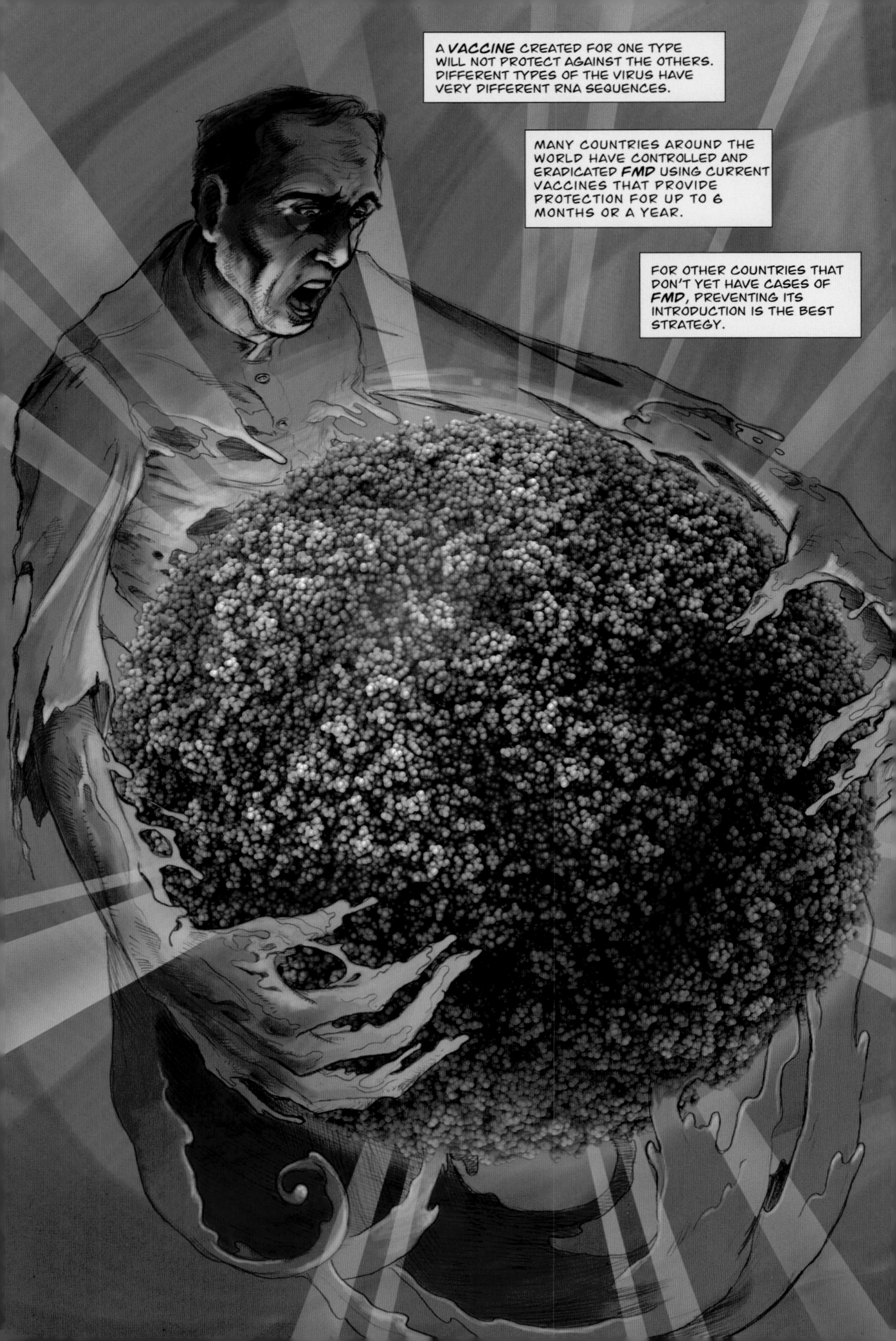
A VACCINE CREATED FOR ONE TYPE WILL NOT PROTECT AGAINST THE OTHERS. DIFFERENT TYPES OF THE VIRUS HAVE VERY DIFFERENT RNA SEQUENCES.
MANY COUNTRIES AROUND THE WORLD HAVE CONTROLLED AND ERADICATED FMD USING CURRENT VACCINES THAT PROVIDE PROTECTION FOR UP TO 6 MONTHS OR A YEAR.
FOR OTHER COUNTRIES THAT DON'T YET HAVE CASES OF FMD, PREVENTING ITS INTRODUCTION IS THE BEST STRATEGY.

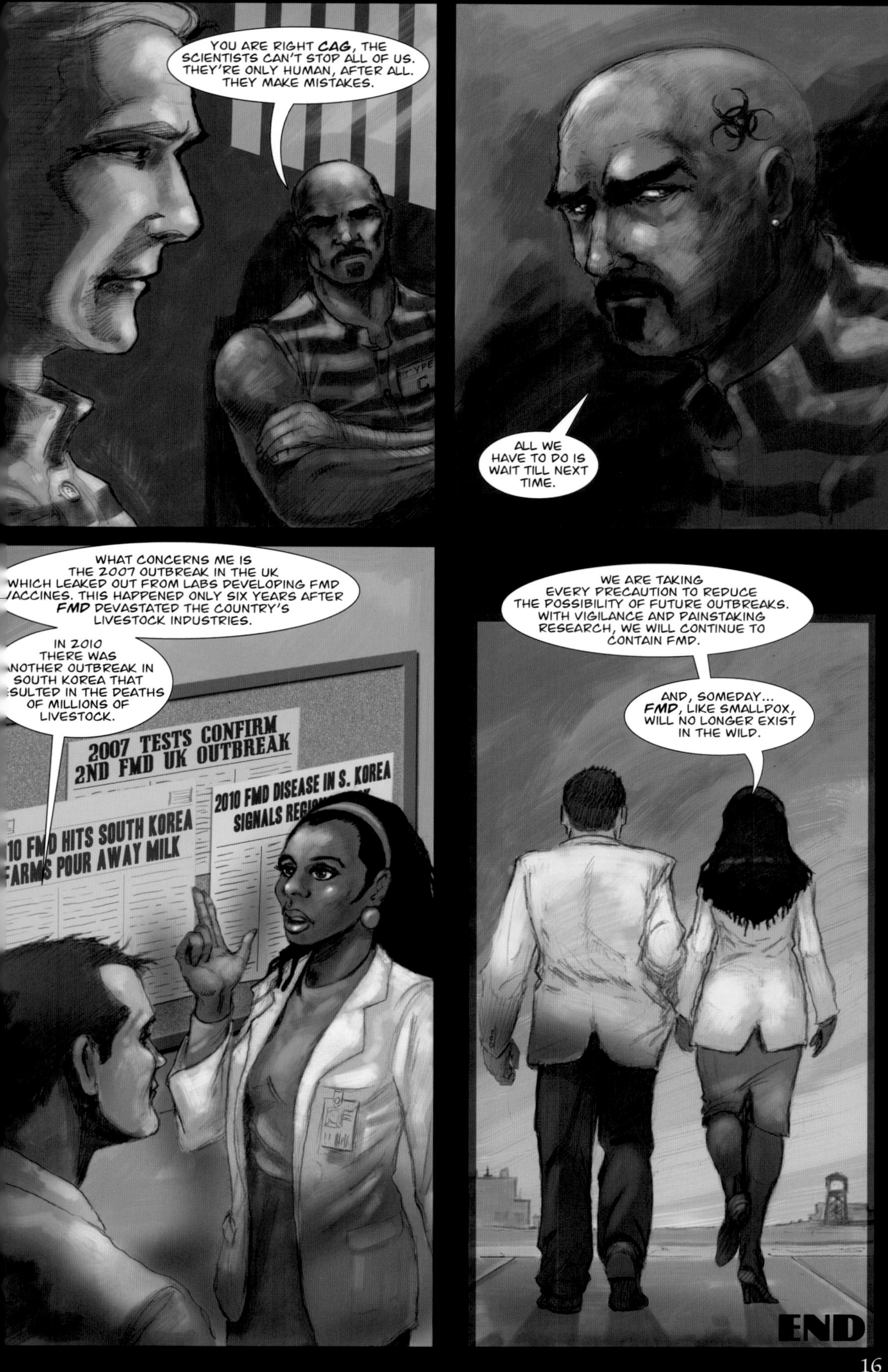

YOU ARE RIGHT CAG, THE SCIENTISTS CAN'T STOP ALL OF US. THEY'RE ONLY HUMAN, AFTER ALL. THEY MAKE MISTAKES.
ALL WE HAVE TO DO IS WAIT TILL NEXT TIME.
WHAT CONCERNS ME IS THE 2007 OUTBREAK IN THE UK WHICH LEAKED OUT FROM LABS DEVELOPING FMD VACCINES. THIS HAPPENED ONLY SIX YEARS AFTER FMD DEVASTATED THE COUNTRY'S LIVESTOCK INDUSTRIES.
IN 2010 THERE WAS ANOTHER OUTBREAK IN SOUTH KOREA THAT RESULTED IN THE DEATHS OF MILLIONS OF LIVESTOCK.
2007 TESTS CONFIRM 2ND FMD UK OUTBREAK
2010 FMD DISEASE IN S. KOREA SIGNALS REGIO
10 FMD HITS SOUTH KOREA FARMS POUR AWAY MILK
WE ARE TAKING EVERY PRECAUTION TO REDUCE THE POSSIBILITY OF FUTURE OUTBREAKS. WITH VIGILANCE AND PAINSTAKING RESEARCH, WE WILL CONTINUE TO CONTAIN FMD.
AND, SOMEDAY... FMD, LIKE SMALLPOX, WILL NO LONGER EXIST IN THE WILD.
END

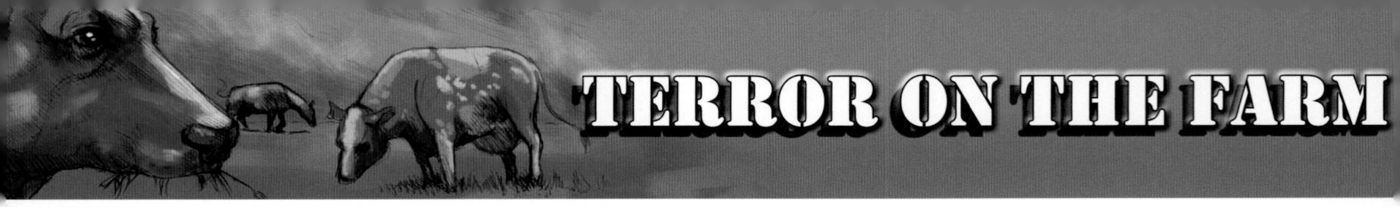

TERROR ON THE FARM

by Ann Downer-Hazell

At the bustling arrivals gate of a busy airport, a highly trained, dedicated agent is on patrol. He weaves his way along the line of passengers waiting to pass through customs. Then he pauses, nose twitching.

Our special agent is a beagle.

This sniffer dog has been using his sensitive nose to "search" disembarking passengers and their luggage. He is on the lookout not for drugs or bombs but for meat barred from entry into the United States.

Have family members ever brought a favorite food back from a trip overseas? While a ham or sausage may seem harmless, it has the potential to unleash a threat so powerful it could result in the slaughter of millions of infected animals.

Meat can harbor the FMD virus, the infectious agent that causes foot and mouth disease. People can't get foot and mouth disease, so the meat isn't dangerous to us. When meat scraps end up in pig food, however, FMD virus can end up in animals. There isn't any FMD virus in the United States. Because customs officials want to keep it that way, they have a "search and destroy" mission for meat products from countries where FMD virus exists.

This highly contagious virus targets mammals with cloven hoofs, including cattle, pigs, sheep, and goats as well as wild animals like deer and bison. Some animals carry the virus without getting sick, while others develop the disease. Infected animals soon develop a fever and painful blisters in the mouth and on their feet. Animals that recover remain infected—and contagious. Spread through the air, from animal to animal, or by equipment and vehicles, the virus can move rapidly from farm to farm. Because it is one of the most infectious viruses known, virus-free countries like the U.S. and Australia have strict regulations to keep potentially infected meat out.

FMD virus is so dangerous that scientists can only study it in high-security labs. Only one lab in the U.S. is secure enough to contain the FMD virus: the Plum Island Animal Disease Center off the coast of Long Island, New York. Used during World War II to keep a lookout for German submarines, the 840-acre island was converted in 1954 to a secret U.S. Department of Agriculture lab. Its mission: to research diseases like FMD that could threaten American livestock. No longer secret, the lab at Plum Island remains high security, run by the Department of Homeland Security. Here, scientists work to develop better vaccines against different types of the FMD virus.

Scientists need better vaccines because the FMD virus is always changing. Viruses have molecules on their surface that they use to "pick the lock" of the cell they infect. Virologists have learned there are seven types, each with a slightly different set of "lock picks" and each originally identified in a different part of the world. The seven main types are O, A, C, Asia 1, SAT 1, SAT 2, and SAT 3. Now all seven types are found in different places around the world, often far from where they were first isolated and named.

Foot and mouth disease struck the United Kingdom in 2001. By the time the outbreak was brought under control, seven million sheep and cattle had been destroyed at a cost of $16 billion. Six years later, foot and mouth disease struck in the U.K. once more, infecting sixty cows on a farm in Surrey. This time a different strain of FMD virus was responsible, a strain researchers had last seen during an outbreak in the 1960s. This strain was now confined to research labs, like the high-security lab run by the British government at Pirbright. Researchers there concluded with horror that the 2007 cluster of cases had originated at their own lab. Investigators found that the virus had escaped through faulty drainage pipes, infecting animals grazing in nearby fields.

FMD virus cropped up again in South Korea in the fall of 2010. By early 2011, authorities had vaccinated up to 12 million animals and killed another 2 million as they desperately tried to contain the epidemic. By the time the outbreak was over, South Korea had spent $1.6 billion to vaccinate herds, kill infected animals, and disinfect farms.

Could such an outbreak strike in a country like the United States? Researchers in high-security labs are working to develop new and better vaccines. Because the virus types aren't identical, our best vaccines only protect against a single type of the virus for six months. With better vaccines, scientists hope to protect herds from more types for longer periods.

Until then, the best strategy is vigilance. It's easier to keep FMD virus out of countries than to fight it once it's gotten in. That's why the U.S. and other countries, like Australia, work so hard to get and keep their virus-free status. The U.S. Department of Agriculture and customs officials remain on alert to keep the virus off American soil. So far, they have succeeded.

With better vaccines and security at airports, we may win the war against foot and mouth disease. As more countries become virus-free, FMD virus may even become extinct outside the laboratory, the way the smallpox virus is today.

Human
Immunodeficiency
VIRUS

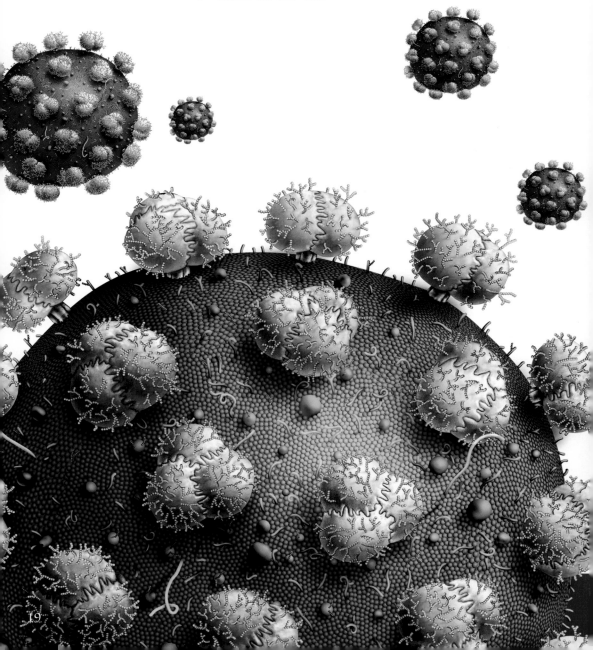

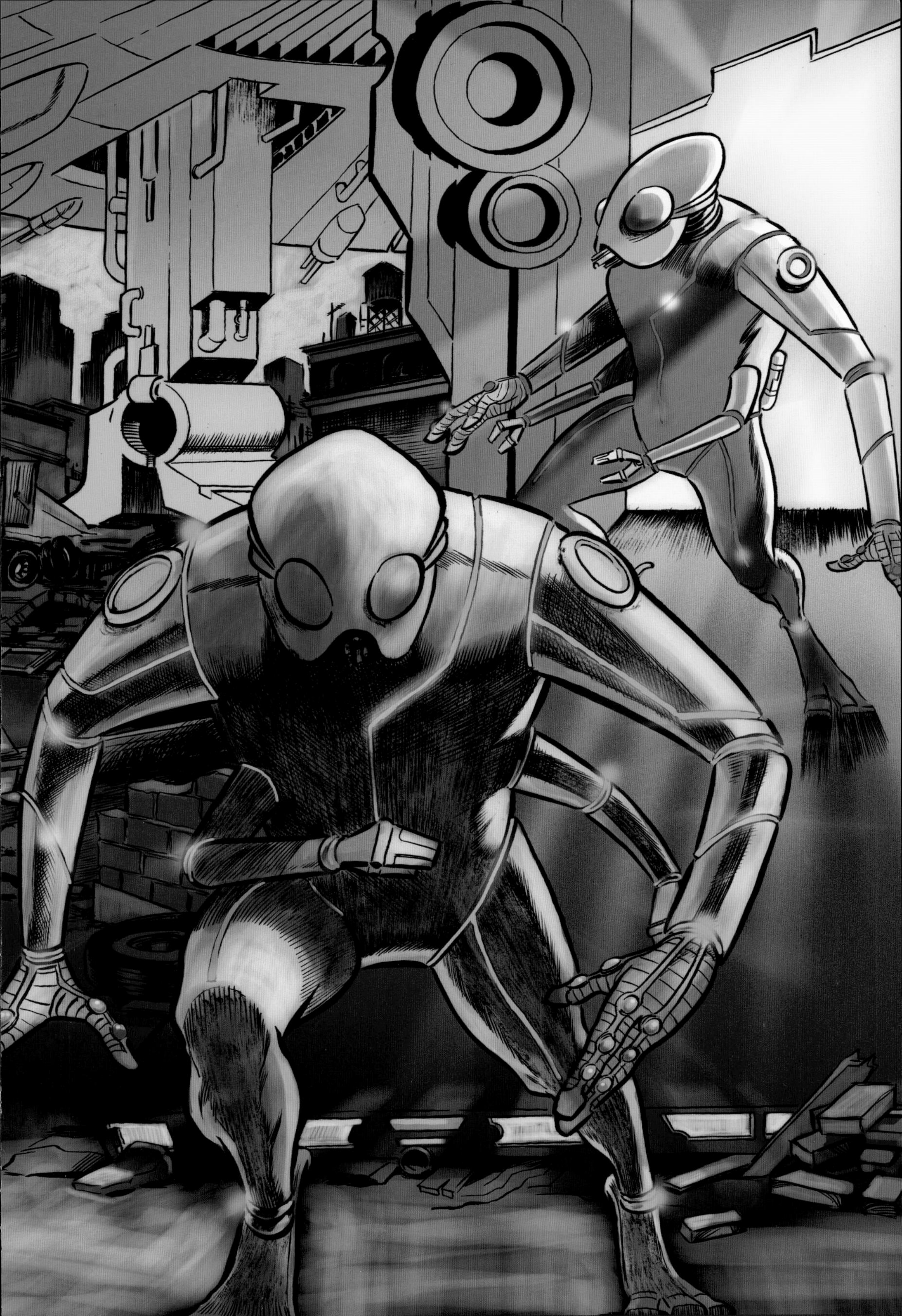

Phantom Planet

Phantom Planet

A MOMENTOUS EVENT.

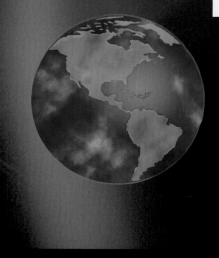

PLANET EARTH, IN THE DISTANT FUTURE,
AS A LONG AWAITED DREAM IS FULFILLED.

AT LAST...*VISITORS FROM OUTER SPACE.*

IT IS AN INCIDENT EPIC IN ITS PROPORTIONS, DEBATED THROUGHOUT THE CENTURIES BY SCIENTISTS AND PHILOSOPHERS.

IT WAS INEVITABLE, MOST PEOPLE BELIEVED, THAT SUCH CONTACT WOULD EVENTUALLY OCCUR.

EVEN SO, WISE SCHOLARS IN THIS WORLD COULD ONLY SPECULATE UPON THE OUTCOME OF SUCH A MEETING. WOULD THESE STRANGE VISITORS BE OUR MORTAL ENEMIES OR OUR NEW-FOUND FRIENDS?

THAT SINGLE TROUBLING QUESTION REMAINED UNANSWERED...

UNTIL *NOW*.

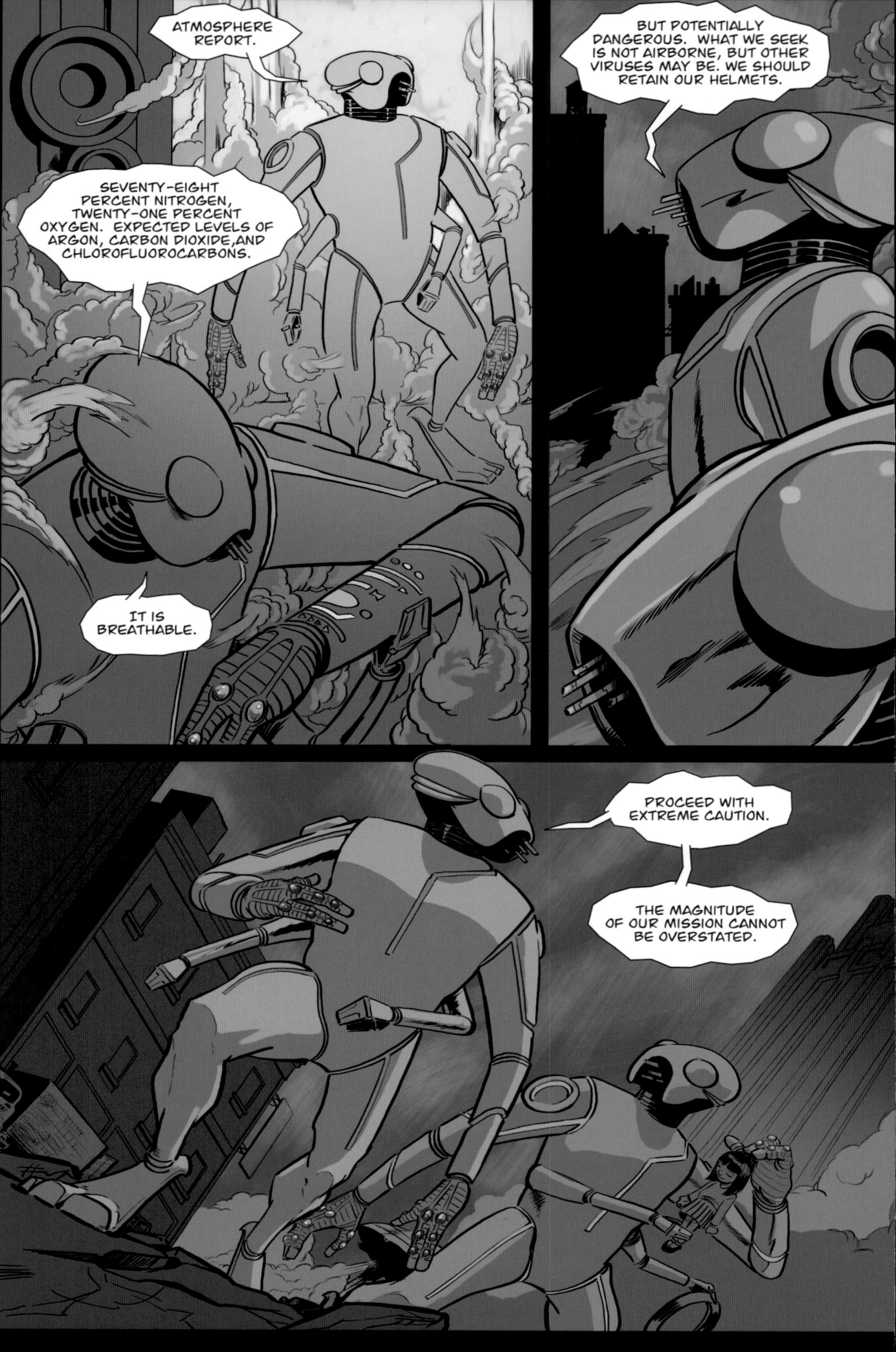
ATMOSPHERE REPORT.
SEVENTY-EIGHT PERCENT NITROGEN, TWENTY-ONE PERCENT OXYGEN. EXPECTED LEVELS OF ARGON, CARBON DIOXIDE,AND CHLOROFLUOROCARBONS.
IT IS BREATHABLE.
BUT POTENTIALLY DANGEROUS. WHAT WE SEEK IS NOT AIRBORNE, BUT OTHER VIRUSES MAY BE. WE SHOULD RETAIN OUR HELMETS.
PROCEED WITH EXTREME CAUTION.
THE MAGNITUDE OF OUR MISSION CANNOT BE OVERSTATED.

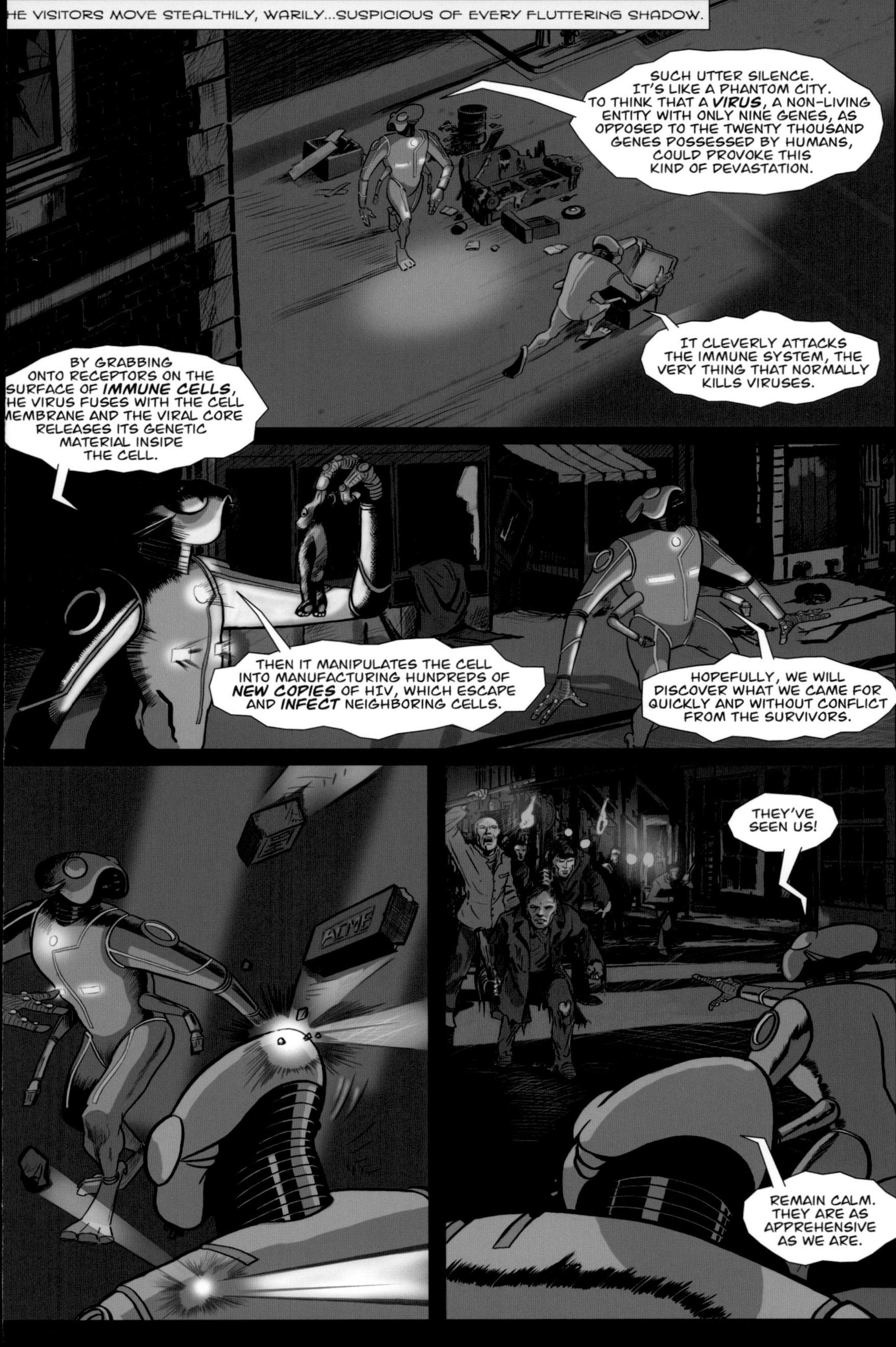

HE VISITORS MOVE STEALTHILY, WARILY...SUSPICIOUS OF EVERY FLUTTERING SHADOW.
SUCH UTTER SILENCE. IT'S LIKE A PHANTOM CITY. TO THINK THAT A VIRUS, A NON-LIVING ENTITY WITH ONLY NINE GENES, AS OPPOSED TO THE TWENTY THOUSAND GENES POSSESSED BY HUMANS, COULD PROVOKE THIS KIND OF DEVASTATION.
IT CLEVERLY ATTACKS THE IMMUNE SYSTEM, THE VERY THING THAT NORMALLY KILLS VIRUSES.
BY GRABBING ONTO RECEPTORS ON THE SURFACE OF IMMUNE CELLS, HE VIRUS FUSES WITH THE CELL EMBRANE AND THE VIRAL CORE RELEASES ITS GENETIC MATERIAL INSIDE THE CELL.
THEN IT MANIPULATES THE CELL INTO MANUFACTURING HUNDREDS OF NEW COPIES OF HIV, WHICH ESCAPE AND INFECT NEIGHBORING CELLS.
HOPEFULLY, WE WILL DISCOVER WHAT WE CAME FOR QUICKLY AND WITHOUT CONFLICT FROM THE SURVIVORS.
ACME
THEY'VE SEEN US!
REMAIN CALM. THEY ARE AS APPREHENSIVE AS WE ARE.

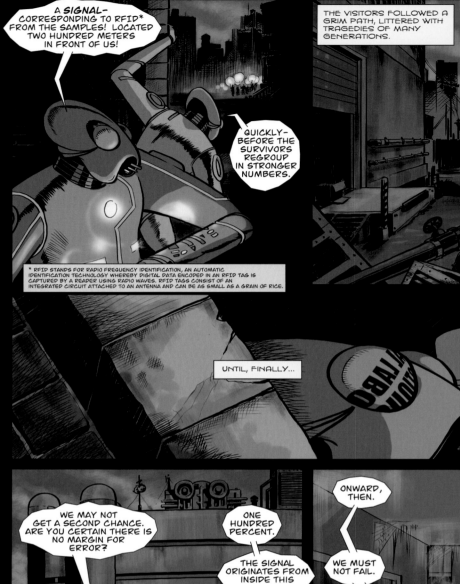

A SIGNAL—CORRESPONDING TO RFID* FROM THE SAMPLES! LOCATED TWO HUNDRED METERS IN FRONT OF US!

QUICKLY—BEFORE THE SURVIVORS REGROUP IN STRONGER NUMBERS.

THE VISITORS FOLLOWED A GRIM PATH, LITTERED WITH TRAGEDIES OF MANY GENERATIONS.

* RFID STANDS FOR RADIO FREQUENCY IDENTIFICATION, AN AUTOMATIC IDENTIFICATION TECHNOLOGY WHEREBY DIGITAL DATA ENCODED IN AN RFID TAG IS CAPTURED BY A READER USING RADIO WAVES. RFID TAGS CONSIST OF AN INTEGRATED CIRCUIT ATTACHED TO AN ANTENNA AND CAN BE AS SMALL AS A GRAIN OF RICE.

UNTIL, FINALLY...

WE MAY NOT GET A SECOND CHANCE. ARE YOU CERTAIN THERE IS NO MARGIN FOR ERROR?

ONE HUNDRED PERCENT.

THE SIGNAL ORIGINATES FROM INSIDE THIS BUILDING.

NATIONAL LABORATORY FOR INFECTIOUS DISEASE

ONWARD, THEN.

WE MUST NOT FAIL.

BSL 2

BSL 3

**BSL2 REFERS TO BIOSAFETY LEVEL TWO, THE MINIMUM LEVEL OF BIOCONTAINMENT REQUIRED TO HOUSE HIV AND SIMILAR BIOLOGICAL AGENTS.
**BSL3 REFERS TO THE BIOSAFETY LEVEL RECOMMENDED FOR HANDLING DANGEROUS PATHOGENS.

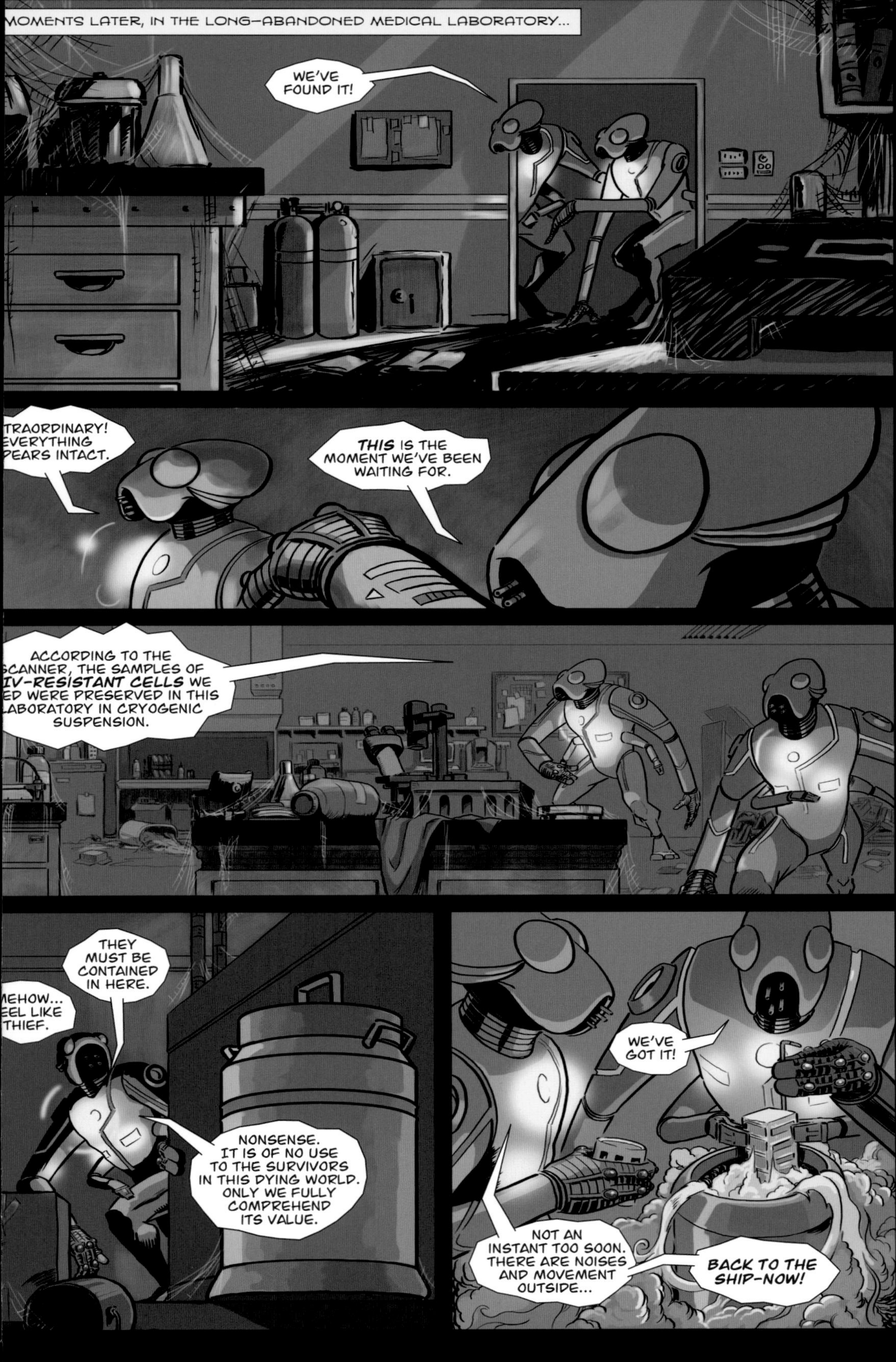
MOMENTS LATER, IN THE LONG-ABANDONED MEDICAL LABORATORY...
WE'VE FOUND IT!
TRAORDINARY! EVERYTHING PEARS INTACT.
THIS IS THE MOMENT WE'VE BEEN WAITING FOR.
ACCORDING TO THE SCANNER, THE SAMPLES OF IV-RESISTANT CELLS WE ED WERE PRESERVED IN THIS LABORATORY IN CRYOGENIC SUSPENSION.
THEY MUST BE CONTAINED IN HERE.
MEHOW... EEL LIKE THIEF.
NONSENSE. IT IS OF NO USE TO THE SURVIVORS IN THIS DYING WORLD. ONLY WE FULLY COMPREHEND ITS VALUE.
WE'VE GOT IT!
NOT AN INSTANT TOO SOON. THERE ARE NOISES AND MOVEMENT OUTSIDE...
BACK TO THE SHIP—NOW!

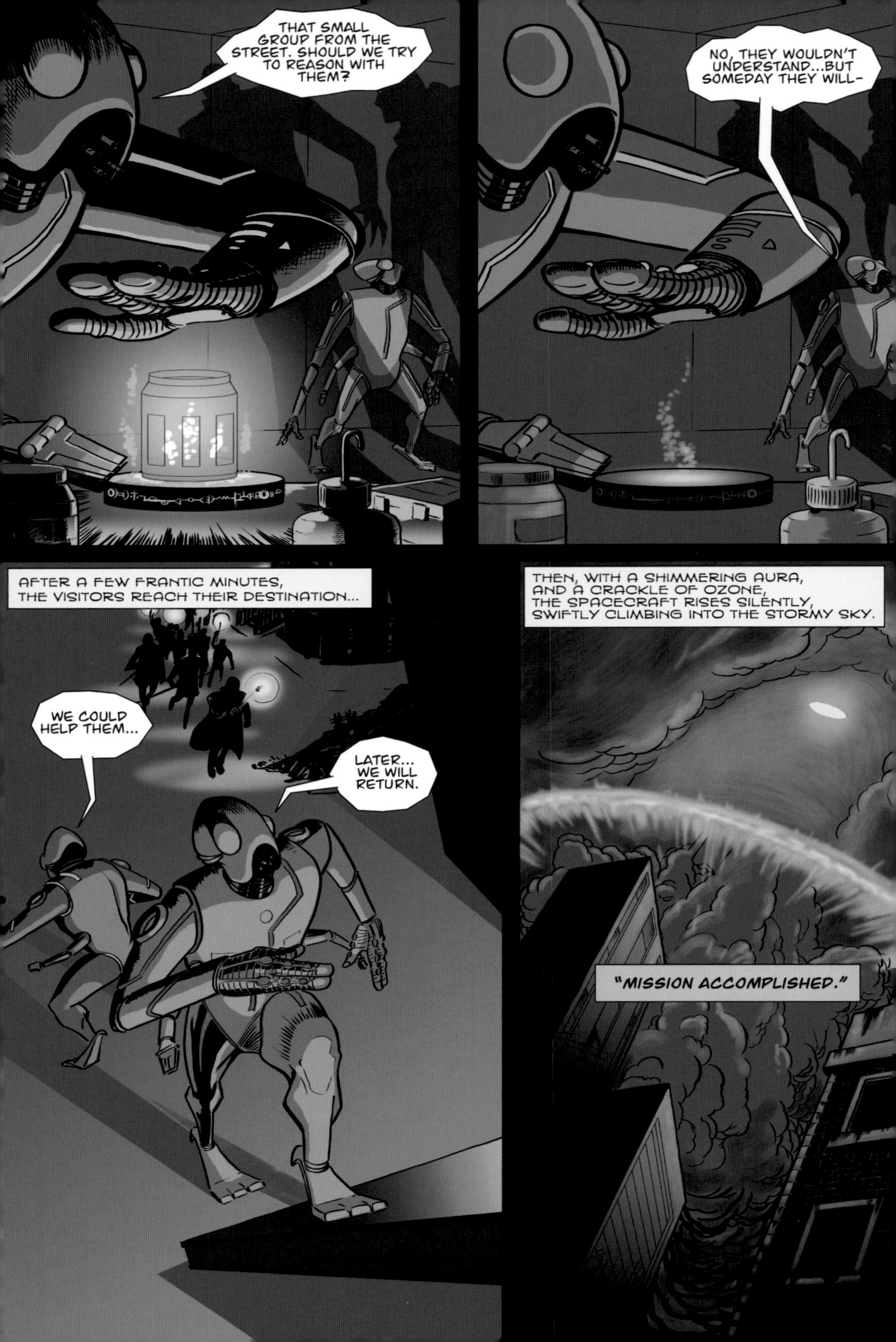
THAT SMALL GROUP FROM THE STREET. SHOULD WE TRY TO REASON WITH THEM?
NO, THEY WOULDN'T UNDERSTAND...BUT SOMEDAY THEY WILL-
AFTER A FEW FRANTIC MINUTES, THE VISITORS REACH THEIR DESTINATION...
WE COULD HELP THEM...
LATER... WE WILL RETURN.
THEN, WITH A SHIMMERING AURA, AND A CRACKLE OF OZONE, THE SPACECRAFT RISES SILENTLY, SWIFTLY CLIMBING INTO THE STORMY SKY.
"MISSION ACCOMPLISHED."

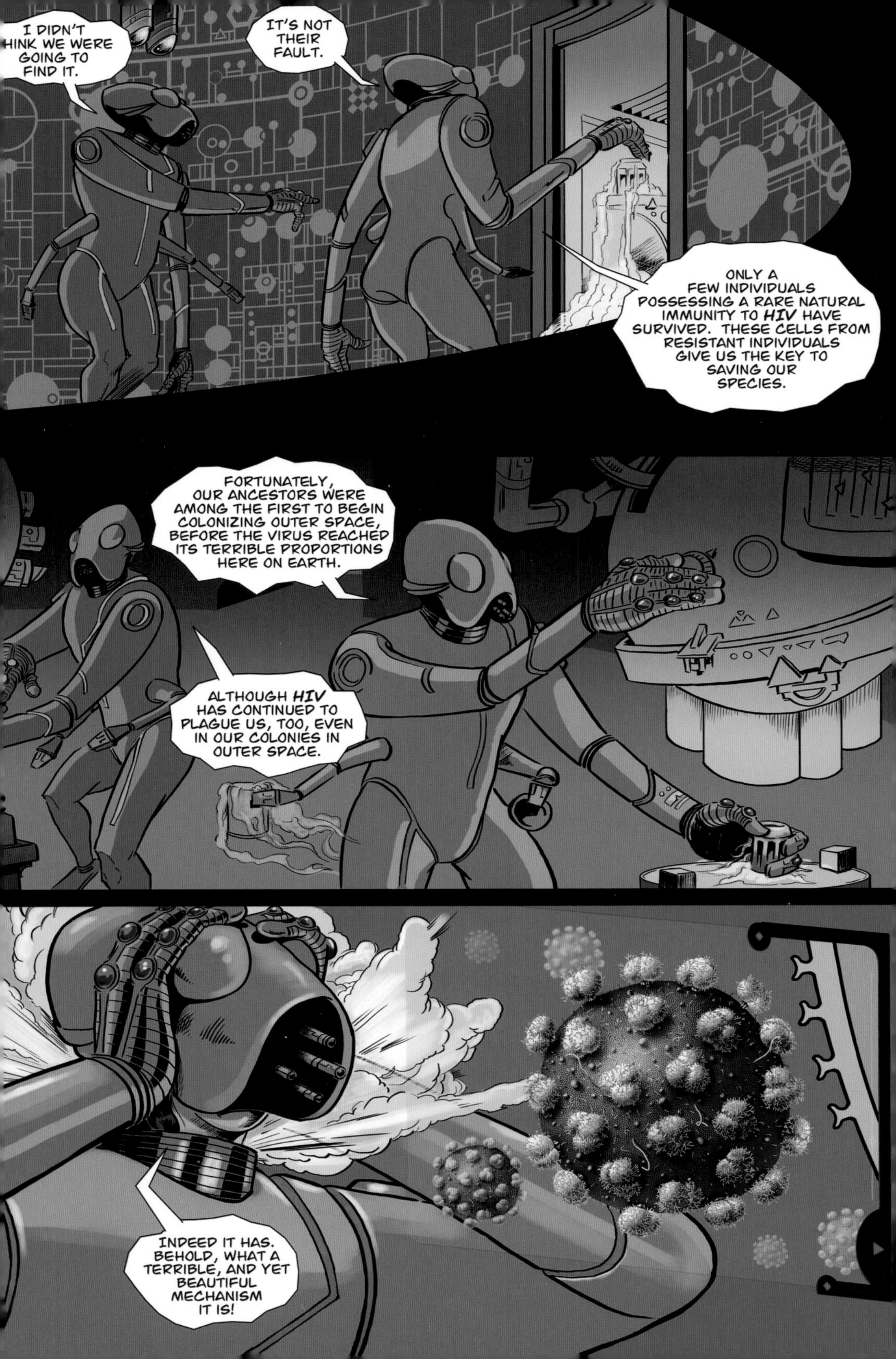
I DIDN'T HINK WE WERE GOING TO FIND IT.
IT'S NOT THEIR FAULT.
ONLY A FEW INDIVIDUALS POSSESSING A RARE NATURAL IMMUNITY TO HIV HAVE SURVIVED. THESE CELLS FROM RESISTANT INDIVIDUALS GIVE US THE KEY TO SAVING OUR SPECIES.
FORTUNATELY, OUR ANCESTORS WERE AMONG THE FIRST TO BEGIN COLONIZING OUTER SPACE, BEFORE THE VIRUS REACHED ITS TERRIBLE PROPORTIONS HERE ON EARTH.
ALTHOUGH HIV HAS CONTINUED TO PLAGUE US, TOO, EVEN IN OUR COLONIES IN OUTER SPACE.
INDEED IT HAS. BEHOLD, WHAT A TERRIBLE, AND YET BEAUTIFUL MECHANISM IT IS!

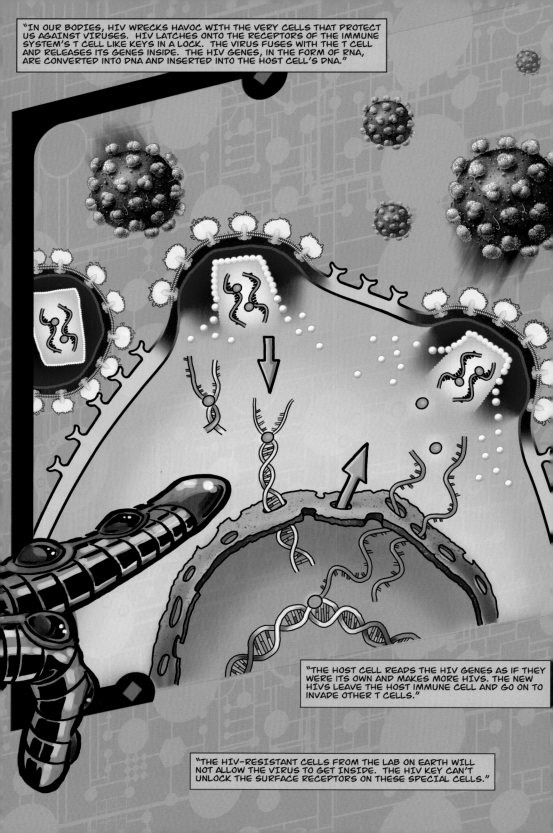

"IN OUR BODIES, HIV WRECKS HAVOC WITH THE VERY CELLS THAT PROTECT US AGAINST VIRUSES. HIV LATCHES ONTO THE RECEPTORS OF THE IMMUNE SYSTEM'S T CELL LIKE KEYS IN A LOCK. THE VIRUS FUSES WITH THE T CELL AND RELEASES ITS GENES INSIDE. THE HIV GENES, IN THE FORM OF RNA, ARE CONVERTED INTO DNA AND INSERTED INTO THE HOST CELL'S DNA."

"THE HOST CELL READS THE HIV GENES AS IF THEY WERE ITS OWN AND MAKES MORE HIVS. THE NEW HIVS LEAVE THE HOST IMMUNE CELL AND GO ON TO INVADE OTHER T CELLS."

"THE HIV-RESISTANT CELLS FROM THE LAB ON EARTH WILL NOT ALLOW THE VIRUS TO GET INSIDE. THE HIV KEY CAN'T UNLOCK THE SURFACE RECEPTORS ON THESE SPECIAL CELLS."

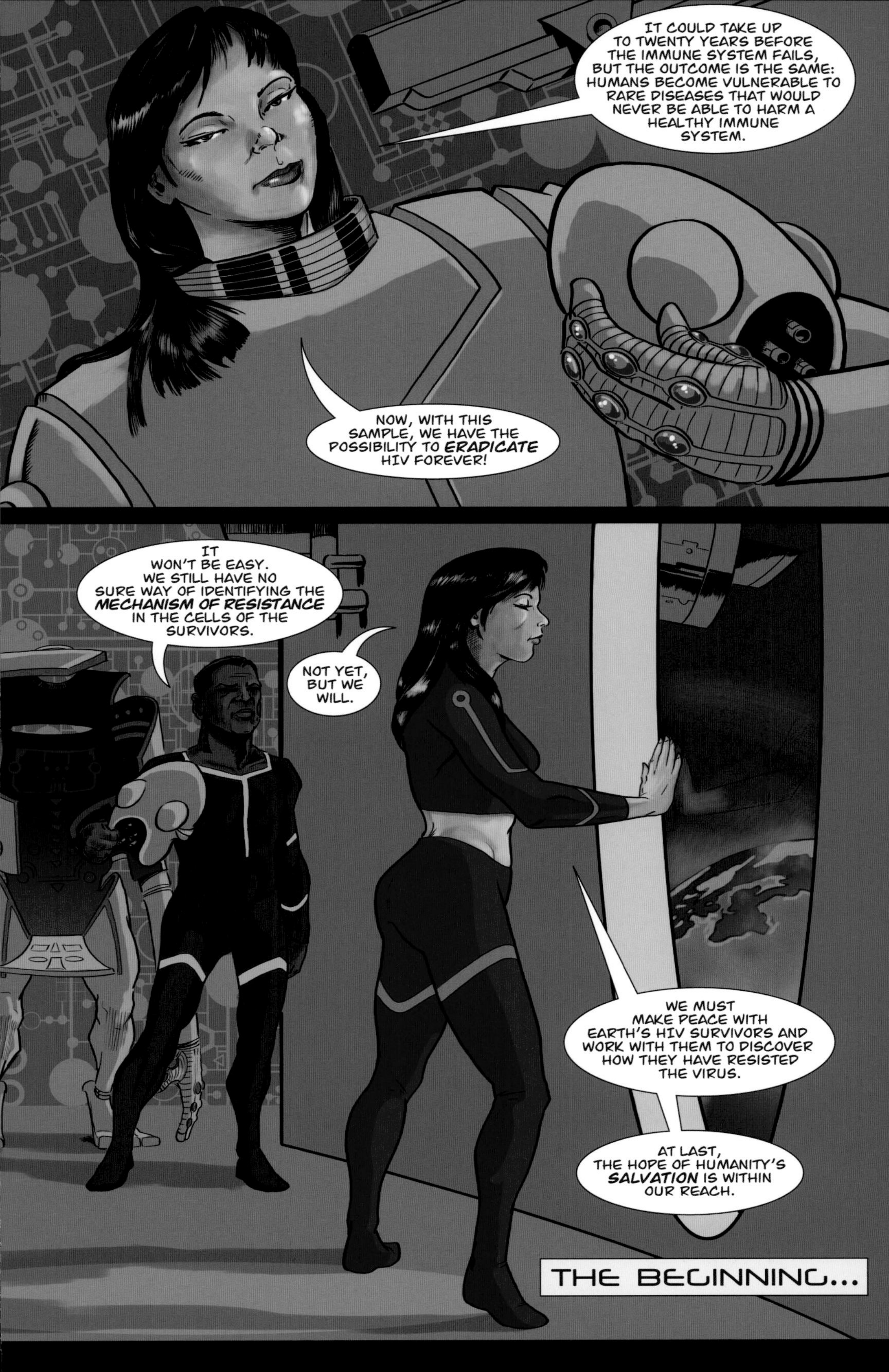
IT COULD TAKE UP TO TWENTY YEARS BEFORE THE IMMUNE SYSTEM FAILS, BUT THE OUTCOME IS THE SAME: HUMANS BECOME VULNERABLE TO RARE DISEASES THAT WOULD NEVER BE ABLE TO HARM A HEALTHY IMMUNE SYSTEM.
NOW, WITH THIS SAMPLE, WE HAVE THE POSSIBILITY TO ERADICATE HIV FOREVER!
IT WON'T BE EASY. WE STILL HAVE NO SURE WAY OF IDENTIFYING THE MECHANISM OF RESISTANCE IN THE CELLS OF THE SURVIVORS.
NOT YET, BUT WE WILL.
WE MUST MAKE PEACE WITH EARTH'S HIV SURVIVORS AND WORK WITH THEM TO DISCOVER HOW THEY HAVE RESISTED THE VIRUS.
AT LAST, THE HOPE OF HUMANITY'S SALVATION IS WITHIN OUR REACH.
THE BEGINNING...

Doomsday Virus

by Ann Downer-Hazell

It's a scenario straight out of science fiction—far in the future, alien astronauts land on Earth only to find its great cities emptied by a global pandemic, humankind all but wiped out by a tiny virus, the human immunodeficiency virus, or HIV.

Viruses are popular sci-fi villains because they seem so, well, alien. If you looked at HIV under a powerful microscope, you'd see a tiny particle, one thousandth the size of one of your own cells. It wears an outer coat of fat studded with protein spikes. Under the fat layer is a protein shell called a capsid. The capsid protects the virus's core, two strands of genetic code in the form of ribonucleic acid, or RNA.

Like other viruses, HIV doesn't appear to be alive. After all, it doesn't grow or eat. It can only reproduce with the aid of a host cell. So how can a tiny particle have the potential to bring a civilization to its knees?

The secret is HIV's ability to slip past the body's defenses. It all starts in the blood stream, when HIV bumps into a white blood cell. Some of our white blood cells have a special protein on their surface called CD4. The protein spikes on HIV fit into CD4 like a key into a lock. Once the virus is attached, its fatty envelope begins to fuse with the membrane of the blood cell. Then it releases its genetic core into the cell.

HIV now takes over the molecular machinery that runs our white blood cells. HIV does this by rewriting its own RNA into DNA. Our cells are unable to tell their own DNA from the virus's DNA, and they begin to carry out the HIV replication instructions. And those instructions tell the cells to make more HIV. As HIV spreads, it kills most of the white blood cells the body uses to fight off disease. At this point, HIV infection becomes the disease AIDS.

Under rare conditions, some people get exposed to HIV but do not get infected. These people have white blood cells with a mutant receptor, one that doesn't allow HIV to enter. The spikes on HIV are unable to lock on to the protein on the cell's membrane and HIV never gets inside the host's white blood cells. Since HIV never hijacks their immune systems, these rare

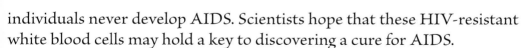

individuals never develop AIDS. Scientists hope that these HIV-resistant white blood cells may hold a key to discovering a cure for AIDS.

Could HIV really make such a doomsday scenario happen? Even if HIV or another virus wiped out millions of people, some members of our species would undoubtedly survive. Somewhere in the survivors' genes would be a mutation—one that provided immunity to the ravages of the virus. If we venture far from Earth to colonize the stars, it's certain viruses will go with us. The mutation that could save us is already written in our genes.

Emiliania huxleyi VIRUS

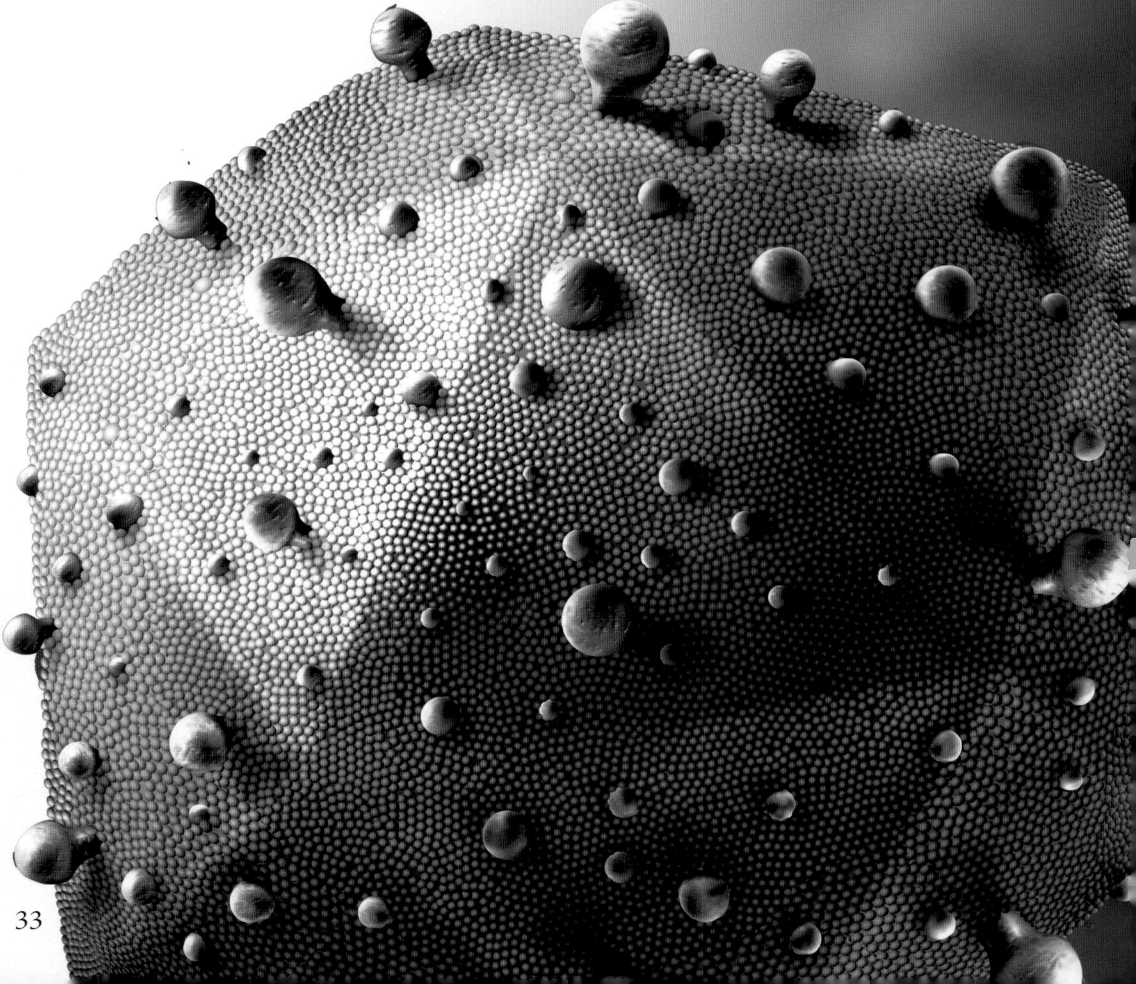

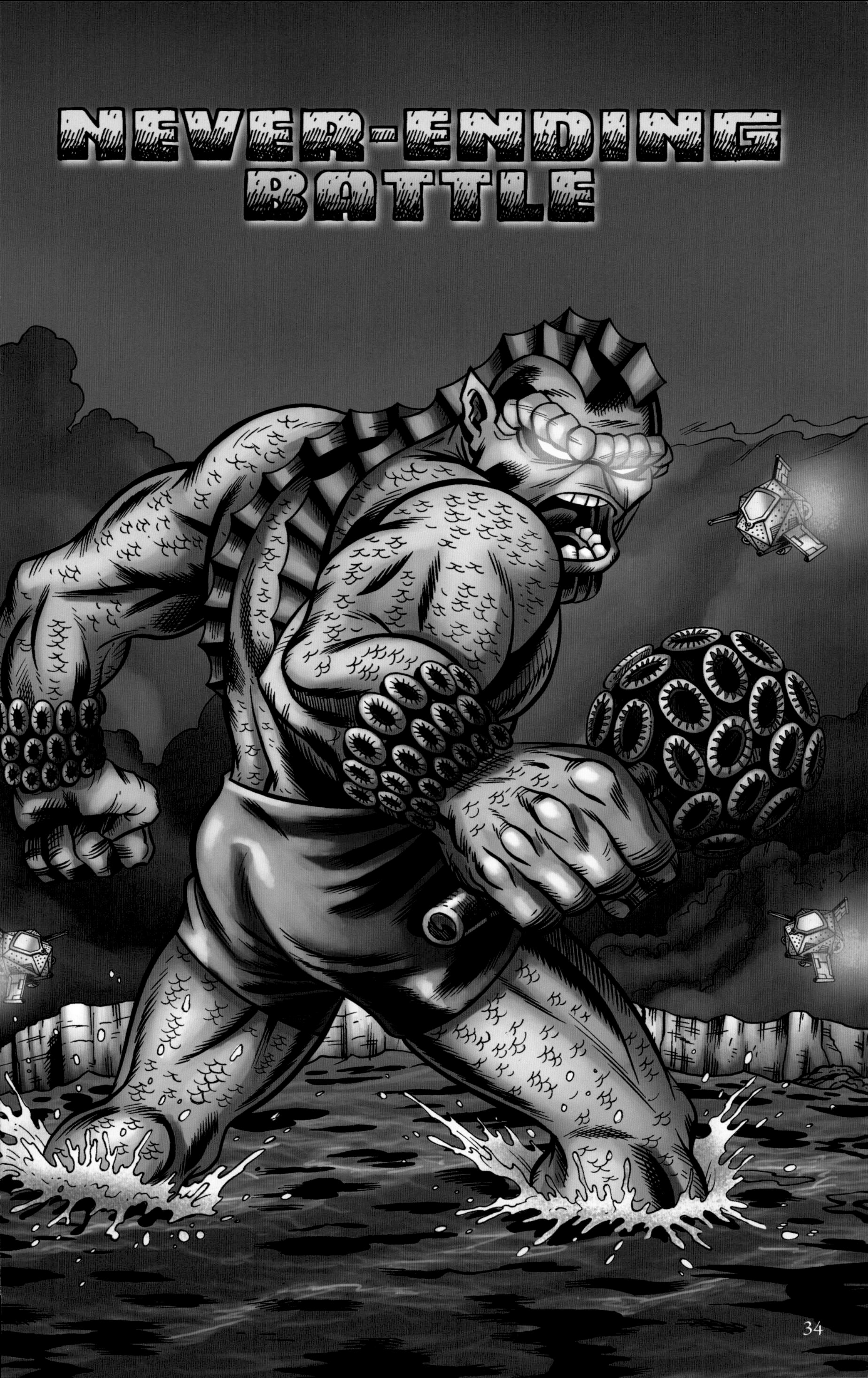
NEVER-ENDING
BATTLE

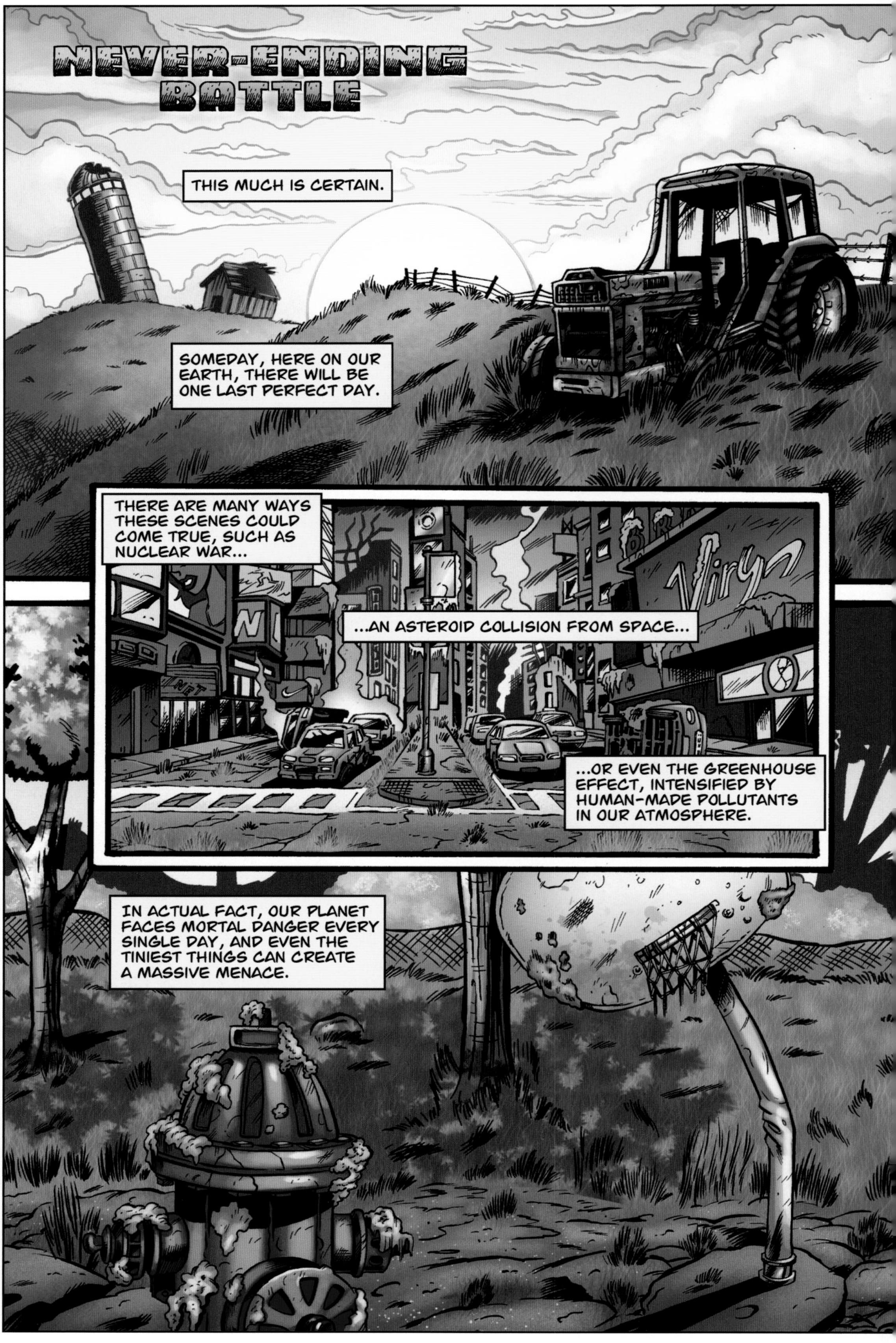
NEVER-ENDING BATTLE
THIS MUCH IS CERTAIN.
SOMEDAY, HERE ON OUR EARTH, THERE WILL BE ONE LAST PERFECT DAY.
THERE ARE MANY WAYS THESE SCENES COULD COME TRUE, SUCH AS NUCLEAR WAR...
...AN ASTEROID COLLISION FROM SPACE...
...OR EVEN THE GREENHOUSE EFFECT, INTENSIFIED BY HUMAN-MADE POLLUTANTS IN OUR ATMOSPHERE.
IN ACTUAL FACT, OUR PLANET FACES MORTAL DANGER EVERY SINGLE DAY, AND EVEN THE TINIEST THINGS CAN CREATE A MASSIVE MENACE.

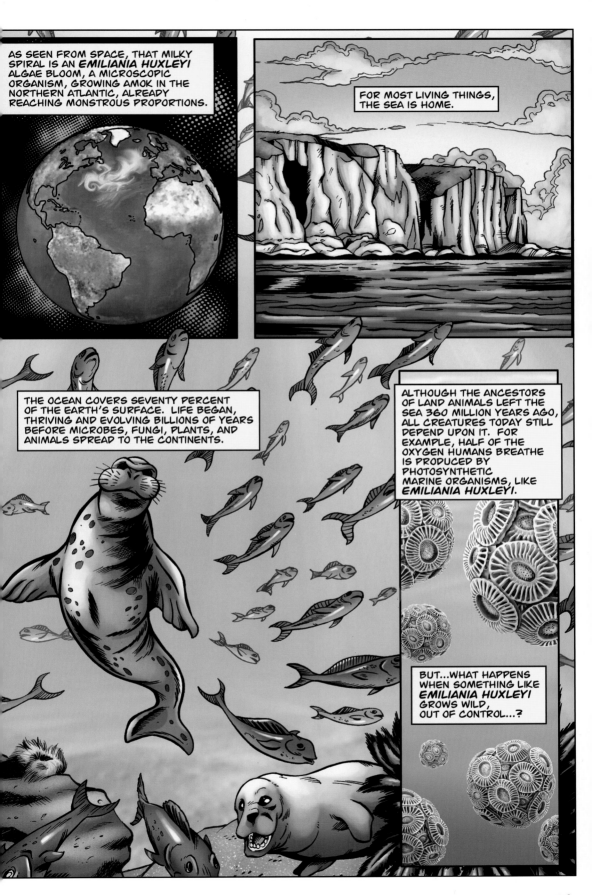

AS SEEN FROM SPACE, THAT MILKY SPIRAL IS AN *EMILIANIA HUXLEYI* ALGAE BLOOM, A MICROSCOPIC ORGANISM, GROWING AMOK IN THE NORTHERN ATLANTIC, ALREADY REACHING MONSTROUS PROPORTIONS.

FOR MOST LIVING THINGS, THE SEA IS HOME.

THE OCEAN COVERS SEVENTY PERCENT OF THE EARTH'S SURFACE. LIFE BEGAN, THRIVING AND EVOLVING BILLIONS OF YEARS BEFORE MICROBES, FUNGI, PLANTS, AND ANIMALS SPREAD TO THE CONTINENTS.

ALTHOUGH THE ANCESTORS OF LAND ANIMALS LEFT THE SEA 360 MILLION YEARS AGO, ALL CREATURES TODAY STILL DEPEND UPON IT. FOR EXAMPLE, HALF OF THE OXYGEN HUMANS BREATHE IS PRODUCED BY PHOTOSYNTHETIC MARINE ORGANISMS, LIKE *EMILIANIA HUXLEYI*.

BUT...WHAT HAPPENS WHEN SOMETHING LIKE *EMILIANIA HUXLEYI* GROWS WILD, OUT OF CONTROL...?

36

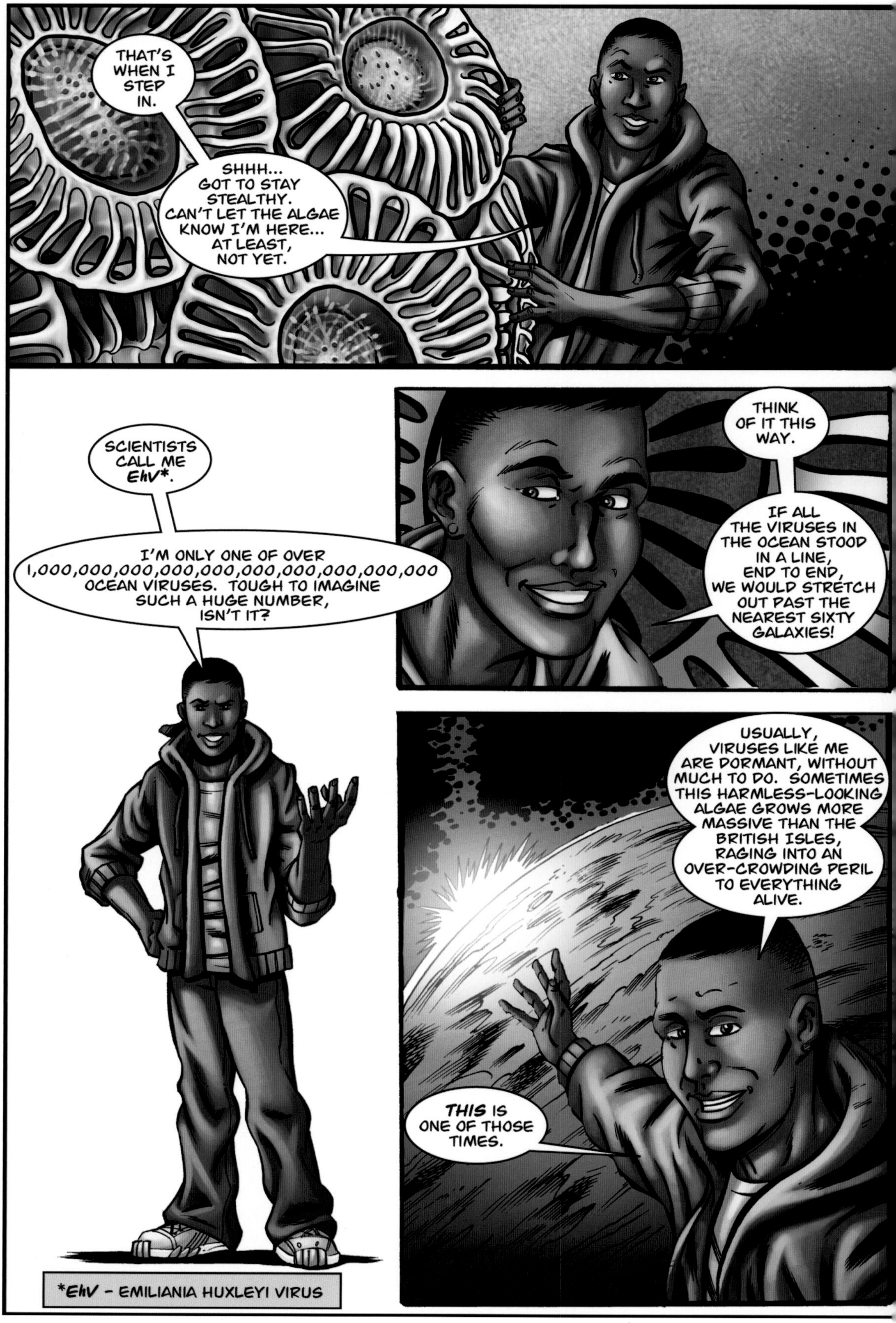

THAT'S WHEN I STEP IN.
SHHH... GOT TO STAY STEALTHY. CAN'T LET THE ALGAE KNOW I'M HERE... AT LEAST, NOT YET.
SCIENTISTS CALL ME *EhV**.
I'M ONLY ONE OF OVER 1,000,000,000,000,000,000,000,000,000,000 OCEAN VIRUSES. TOUGH TO IMAGINE SUCH A HUGE NUMBER, ISN'T IT?
THINK OF IT THIS WAY.
IF ALL THE VIRUSES IN THE OCEAN STOOD IN A LINE, END TO END, WE WOULD STRETCH OUT PAST THE NEAREST SIXTY GALAXIES!
USUALLY, VIRUSES LIKE ME ARE DORMANT, WITHOUT MUCH TO DO. SOMETIMES THIS HARMLESS-LOOKING ALGAE GROWS MORE MASSIVE THAN THE BRITISH ISLES, RAGING INTO AN OVER-CROWDING PERIL TO EVERYTHING ALIVE.
THIS IS ONE OF THOSE TIMES.
*EhV - EMILIANIA HUXLEYI VIRUS

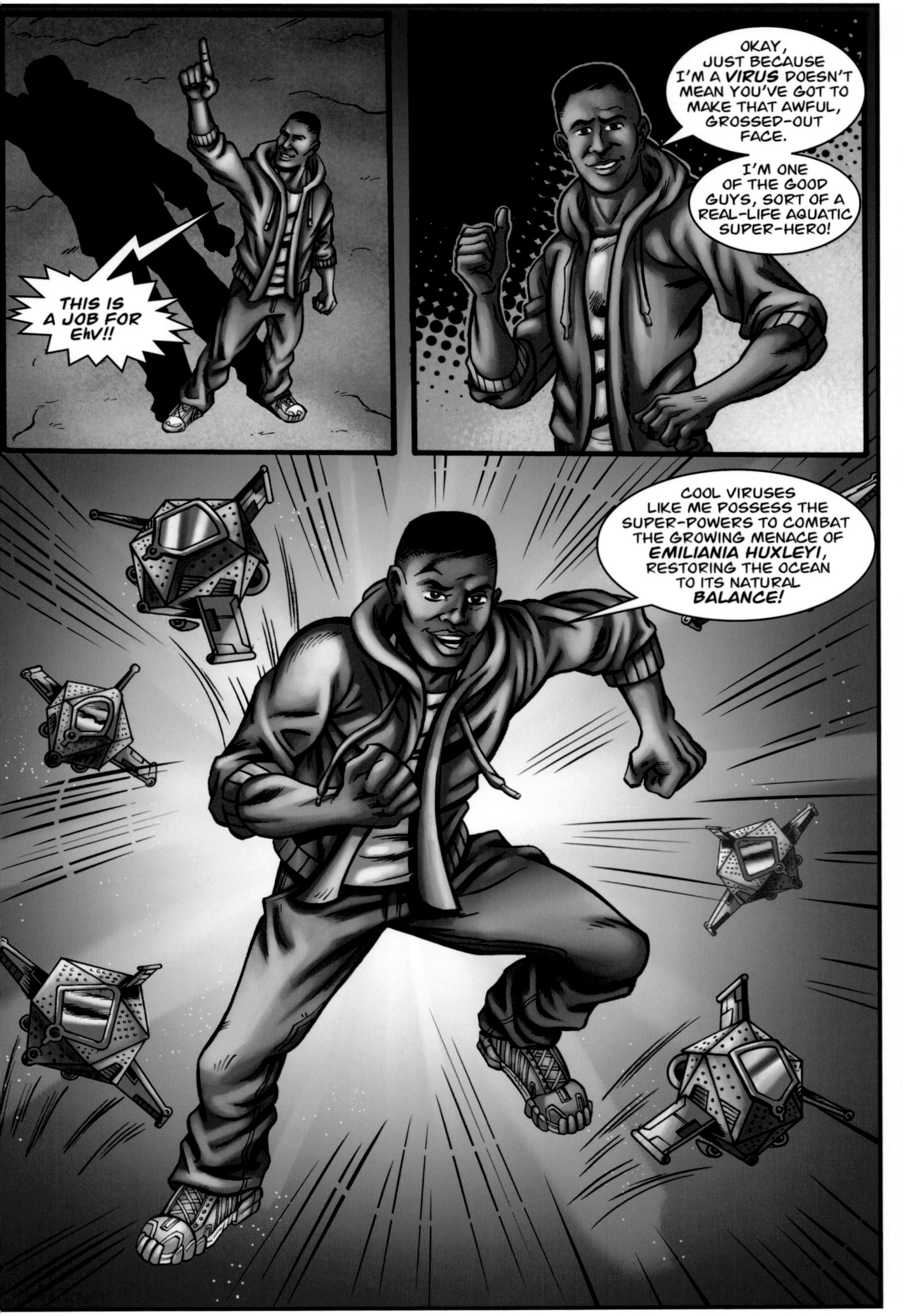
THIS IS A JOB FOR EhV!!
OKAY, JUST BECAUSE I'M A VIRUS DOESN'T MEAN YOU'VE GOT TO MAKE THAT AWFUL, GROSSED-OUT FACE.
I'M ONE OF THE GOOD GUYS, SORT OF A REAL-LIFE AQUATIC SUPER-HERO!
COOL VIRUSES LIKE ME POSSESS THE SUPER-POWERS TO COMBAT THE GROWING MENACE OF EMILIANIA HUXLEYI, RESTORING THE OCEAN TO ITS NATURAL BALANCE!

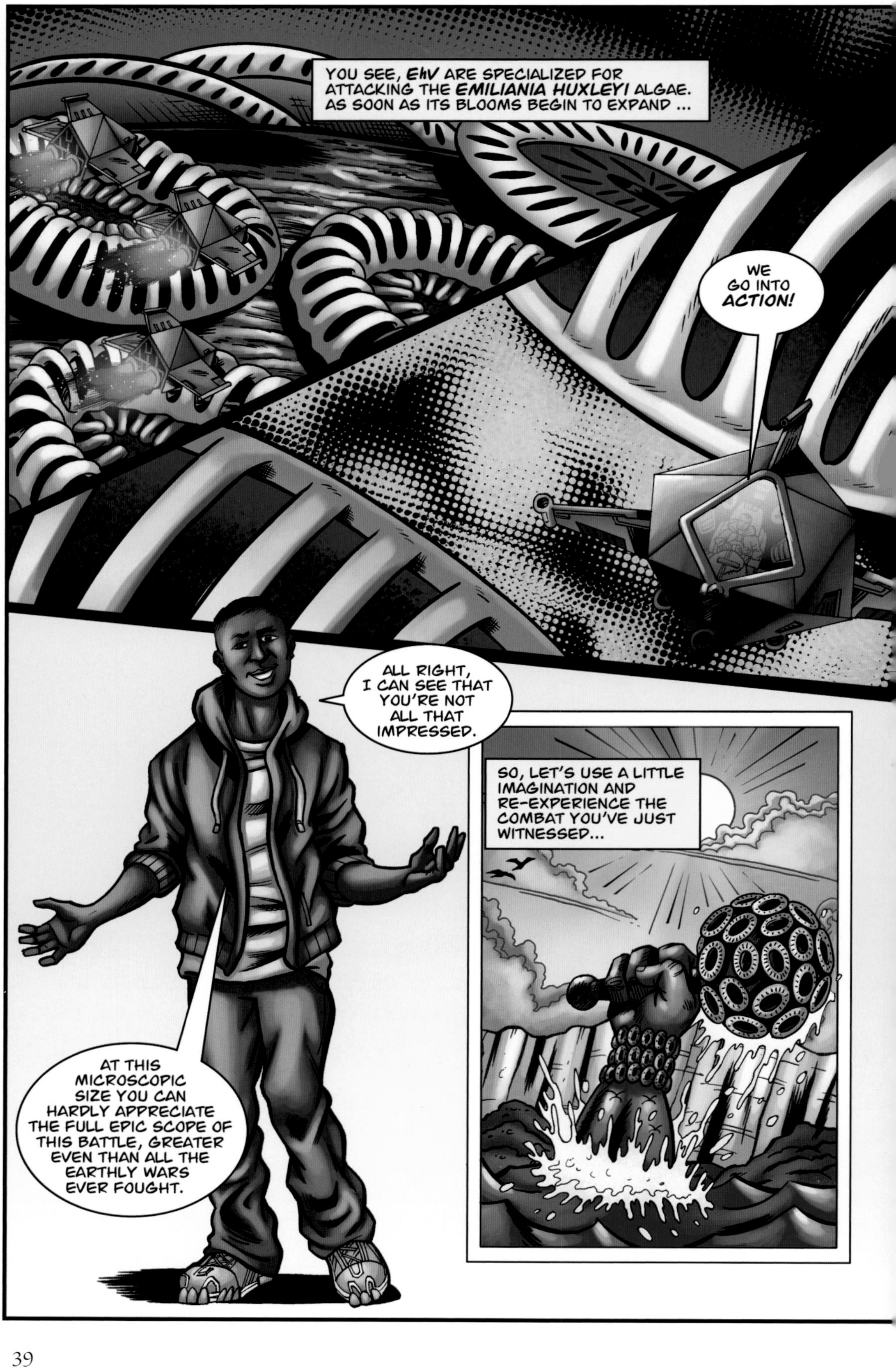
YOU SEE, EhV ARE SPECIALIZED FOR ATTACKING THE EMILIANIA HUXLEYI ALGAE. AS SOON AS ITS BLOOMS BEGIN TO EXPAND ...
WE GO INTO ACTION!
ALL RIGHT, I CAN SEE THAT YOU'RE NOT ALL THAT IMPRESSED.
AT THIS MICROSCOPIC SIZE YOU CAN HARDLY APPRECIATE THE FULL EPIC SCOPE OF THIS BATTLE, GREATER EVEN THAN ALL THE EARTHLY WARS EVER FOUGHT.
SO, LET'S USE A LITTLE IMAGINATION AND RE-EXPERIENCE THE COMBAT YOU'VE JUST WITNESSED...

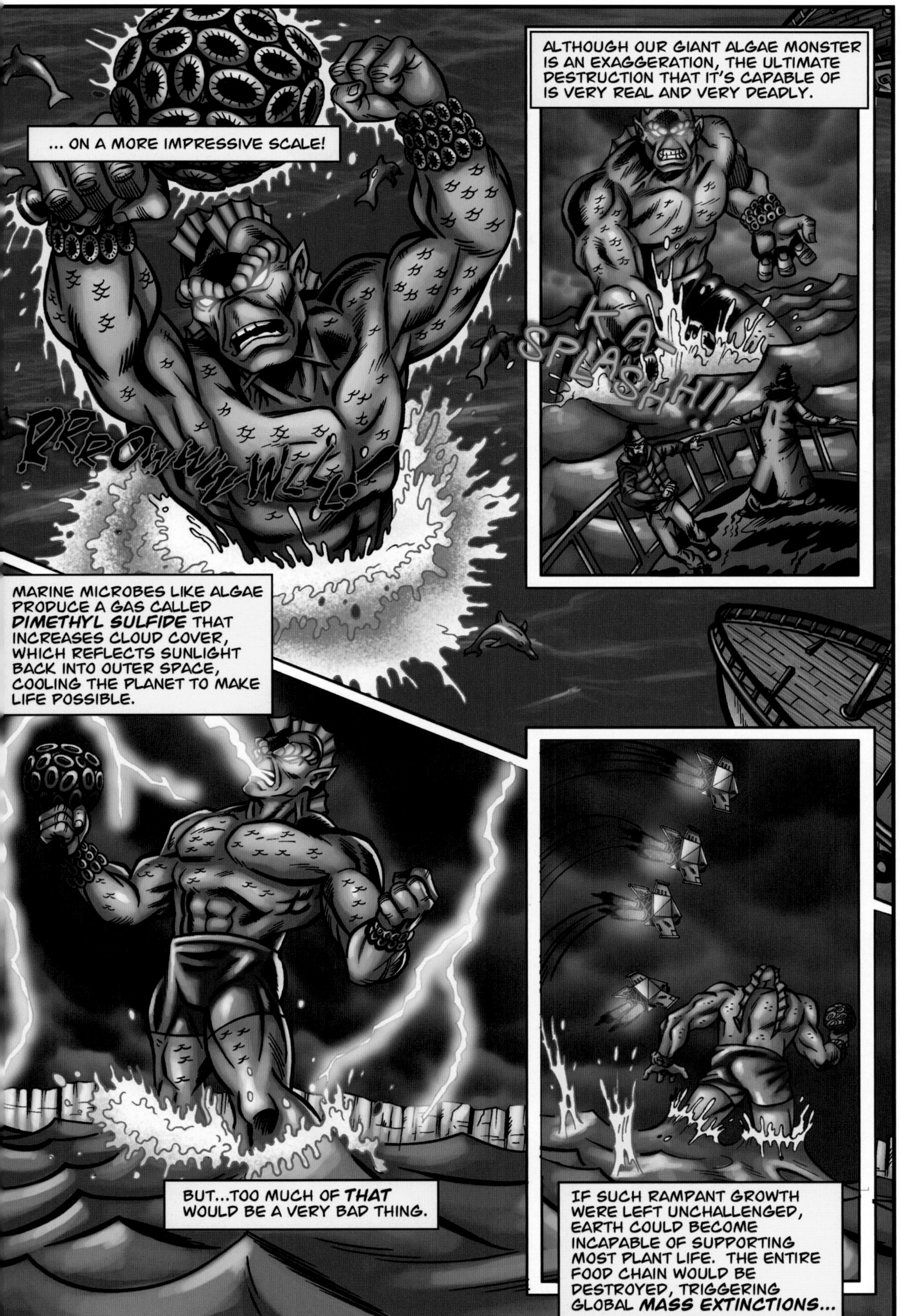

... ON A MORE IMPRESSIVE SCALE!
DRROWWWWLLL!
ALTHOUGH OUR GIANT ALGAE MONSTER IS AN EXAGGERATION, THE ULTIMATE DESTRUCTION THAT IT'S CAPABLE OF IS VERY REAL AND VERY DEADLY.
KA-SPLASHH!!
MARINE MICROBES LIKE ALGAE PRODUCE A GAS CALLED DIMETHYL SULFIDE THAT INCREASES CLOUD COVER, WHICH REFLECTS SUNLIGHT BACK INTO OUTER SPACE, COOLING THE PLANET TO MAKE LIFE POSSIBLE.
BUT...TOO MUCH OF THAT WOULD BE A VERY BAD THING.
IF SUCH RAMPANT GROWTH WERE LEFT UNCHALLENGED, EARTH COULD BECOME INCAPABLE OF SUPPORTING MOST PLANT LIFE. THE ENTIRE FOOD CHAIN WOULD BE DESTROYED, TRIGGERING GLOBAL MASS EXTINCTIONS...

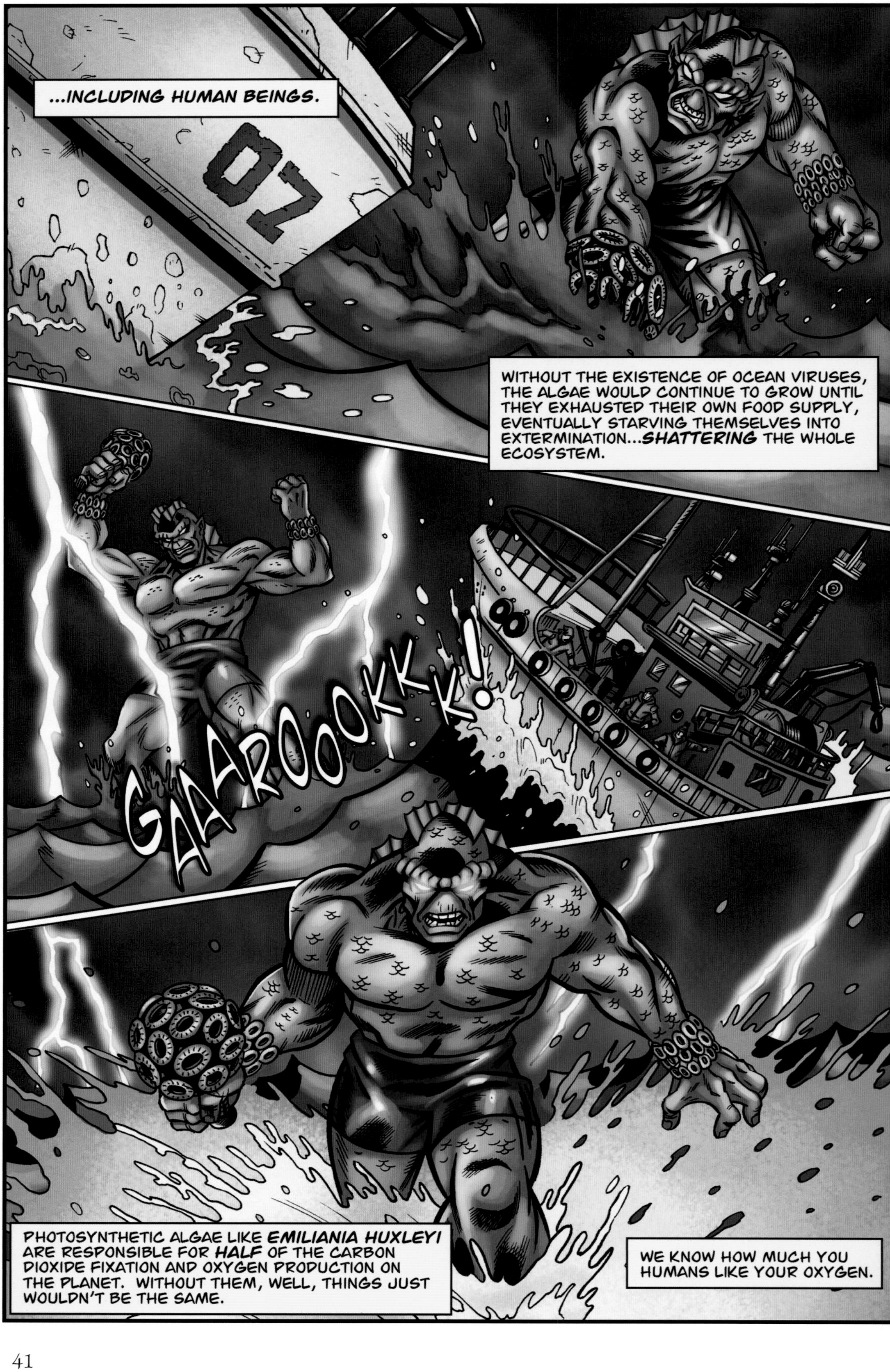
...INCLUDING HUMAN BEINGS.
07
WITHOUT THE EXISTENCE OF OCEAN VIRUSES, THE ALGAE WOULD CONTINUE TO GROW UNTIL THEY EXHAUSTED THEIR OWN FOOD SUPPLY, EVENTUALLY STARVING THEMSELVES INTO EXTERMINATION...SHATTERING THE WHOLE ECOSYSTEM.
GAAROOOKKK!
PHOTOSYNTHETIC ALGAE LIKE EMILIANIA HUXLEYI ARE RESPONSIBLE FOR HALF OF THE CARBON DIOXIDE FIXATION AND OXYGEN PRODUCTION ON THE PLANET. WITHOUT THEM, WELL, THINGS JUST WOULDN'T BE THE SAME.
WE KNOW HOW MUCH YOU HUMANS LIKE YOUR OXYGEN.

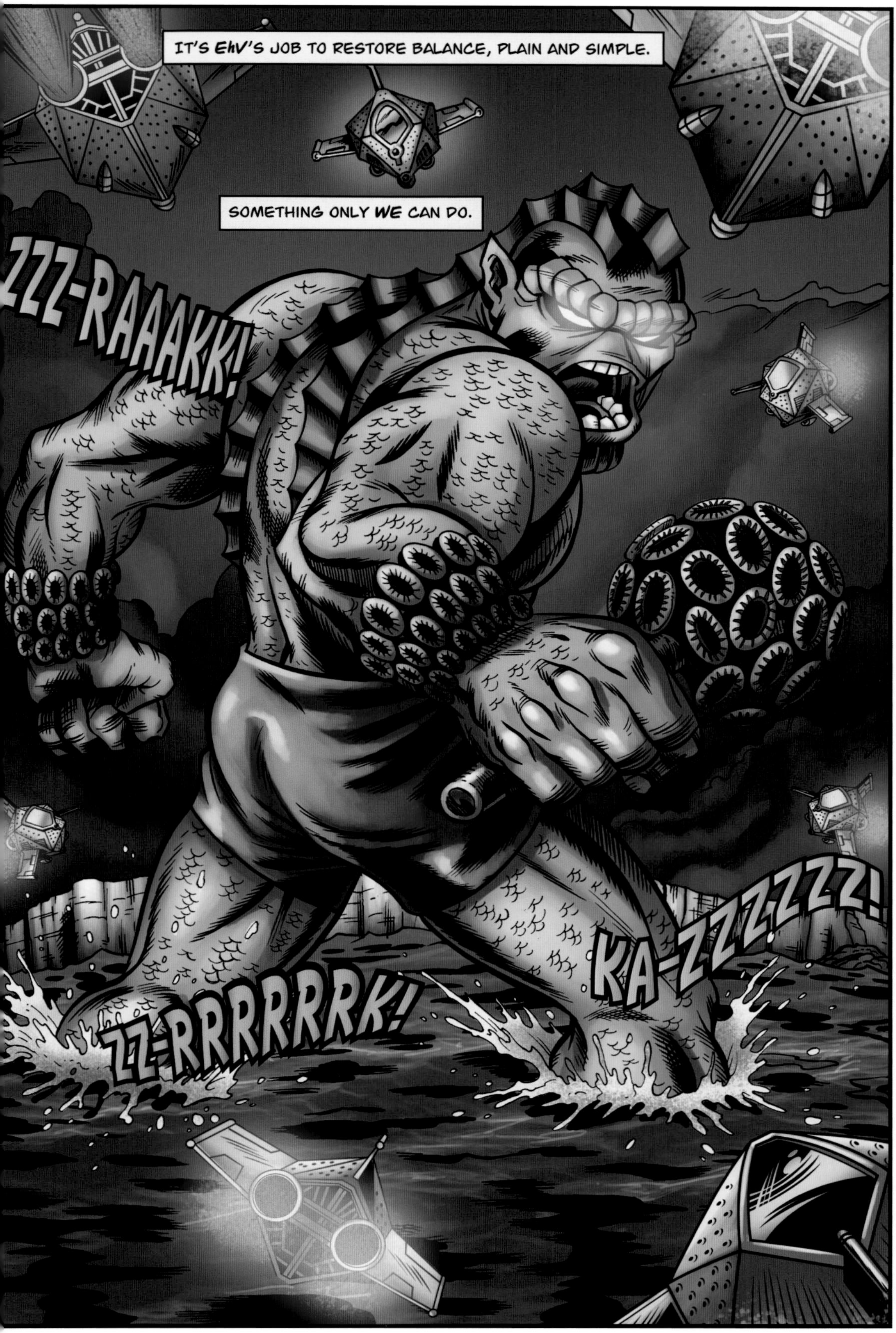
IT'S EhV'S JOB TO RESTORE BALANCE, PLAIN AND SIMPLE.
SOMETHING ONLY WE CAN DO.
ZZZ-RAAAKK!
KA-ZZZZZZZ!
ZZ-RRRRRRK!

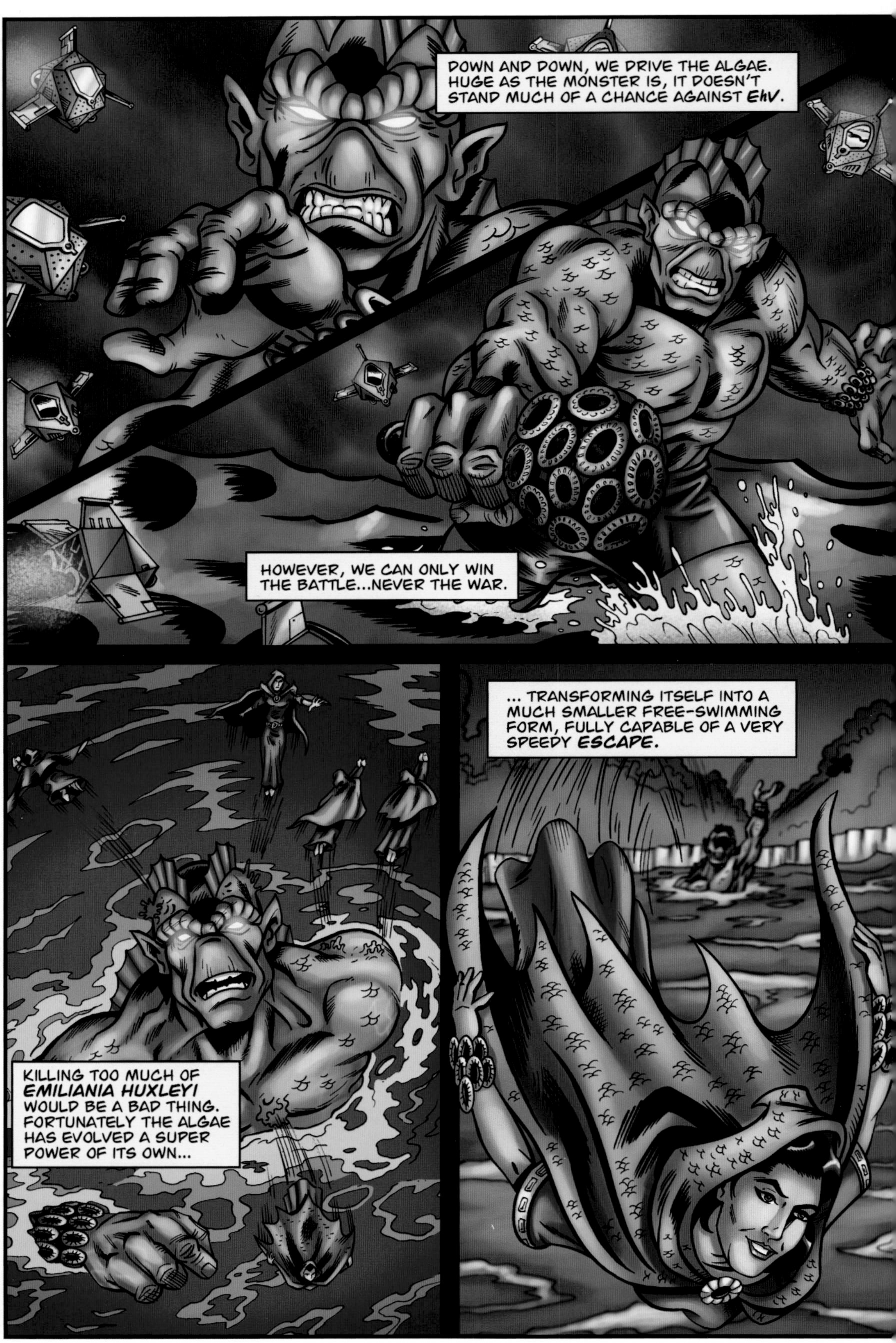
DOWN AND DOWN, WE DRIVE THE ALGAE. HUGE AS THE MONSTER IS, IT DOESN'T STAND MUCH OF A CHANCE AGAINST EhV.
HOWEVER, WE CAN ONLY WIN THE BATTLE...NEVER THE WAR.
KILLING TOO MUCH OF EMILIANIA HUXLEYI WOULD BE A BAD THING. FORTUNATELY THE ALGAE HAS EVOLVED A SUPER POWER OF ITS OWN...
... TRANSFORMING ITSELF INTO A MUCH SMALLER FREE-SWIMMING FORM, FULLY CAPABLE OF A VERY SPEEDY ESCAPE.

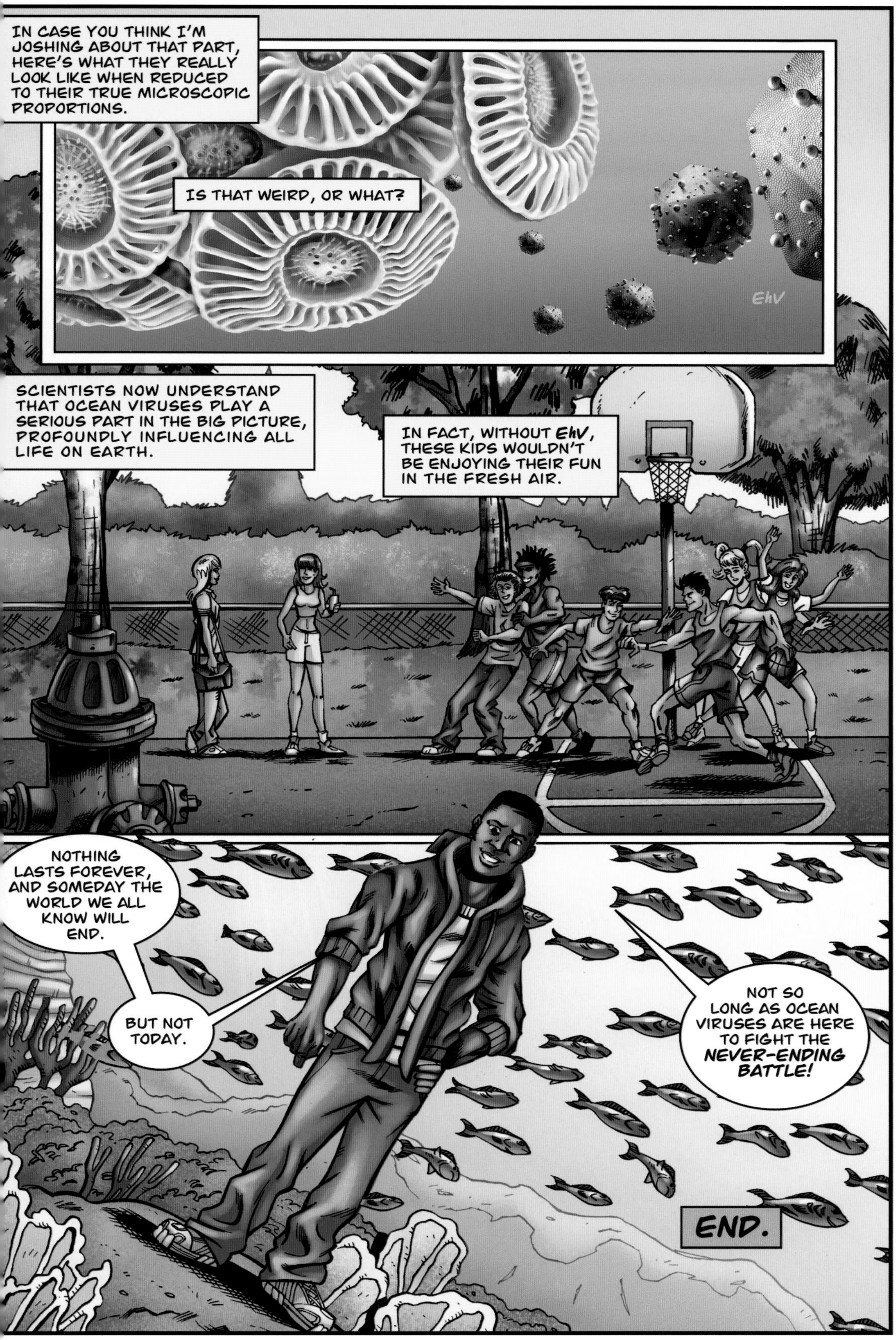
IN CASE YOU THINK I'M JOSHING ABOUT THAT PART, HERE'S WHAT THEY REALLY LOOK LIKE WHEN REDUCED TO THEIR TRUE MICROSCOPIC PROPORTIONS.
IS THAT WEIRD, OR WHAT?
EhV
SCIENTISTS NOW UNDERSTAND THAT OCEAN VIRUSES PLAY A SERIOUS PART IN THE BIG PICTURE, PROFOUNDLY INFLUENCING ALL LIFE ON EARTH.
IN FACT, WITHOUT EhV, THESE KIDS WOULDN'T BE ENJOYING THEIR FUN IN THE FRESH AIR.
NOTHING LASTS FOREVER, AND SOMEDAY THE WORLD WE ALL KNOW WILL END.
BUT NOT TODAY.
NOT SO LONG AS OCEAN VIRUSES ARE HERE TO FIGHT THE NEVER-ENDING BATTLE!
END.

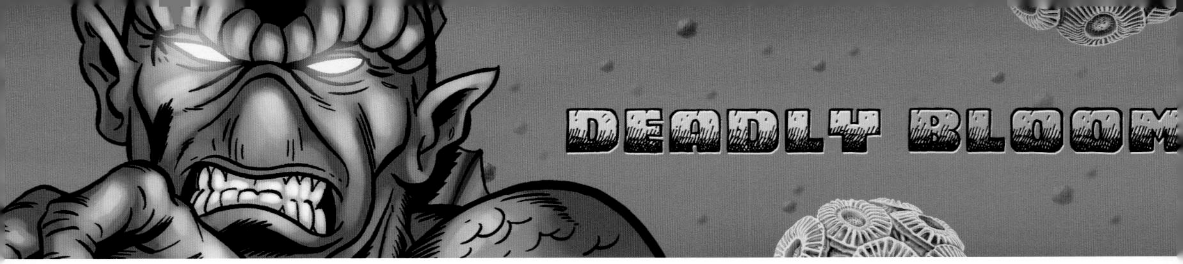

DEADLY BLOOM

by Ann Downer-Hazell

When we imagine an event that could wipe out humankind's reign on Earth, we picture certain apocalyptic scenarios: nuclear winter, an asteroid impact, global warming. Yet every day our planet faces the threat of a different apocalypse from a tiny organism capable of growing into a massive menace.

Emiliania huxleyi is that threat. *E. huxleyi*, as it's known, is a marine alga capable of growing out of control, forming huge "blooms" visible from space as a large, milky spiral stretching hundreds of miles.

Oceans cover seventy percent of the Earth's surface, and they are the engines of life on our planet. Life flourished in the seas for billions of years before microbes and fungi, and plants and animals, spread to the continents. Ancestors of today's land animals left the seas 360 million years ago, but all creatures still depend on the oxygen produced by photosynthetic marine organisms like E. *huxleyi*. Sometimes, however, *E. huxleyi* grows out of control.

Marine algae like *E. huxleyi* produce dimethyl sulfide, a gas that increases cloud cover. The clouds reflect some sunlight back into outer space, cooling the planet to a temperature range that makes life possible. But during an *E. huxleyi* outbreak, the increased cloud cover becomes too much of a good thing. If *E. huxleyi* is allowed to grow unchecked, the planet could cool so much it could no longer support most plant life. The global food chain would collapse, resulting in mass extinctions—including our own.

That's when *Emiliania huxleyi* virus (EhV) steps in. EhV is one of one nonillion (1,000,000,000,000,000,000,000,000,000,000) viruses that live in the ocean. To wrap your head around that large a number, imagine all those viruses lined up end to end. The line would stretch out past the next sixty galaxies. EhV is a specialist, adapted to attack one target in particular: *E. huxleyi*. It usually lies dormant until *E. huxleyi* begins to grow out of control, forming a bloom larger than the British Isles. As soon as the bloom begins to expand, EhV goes into attack mode, driving the algae down.

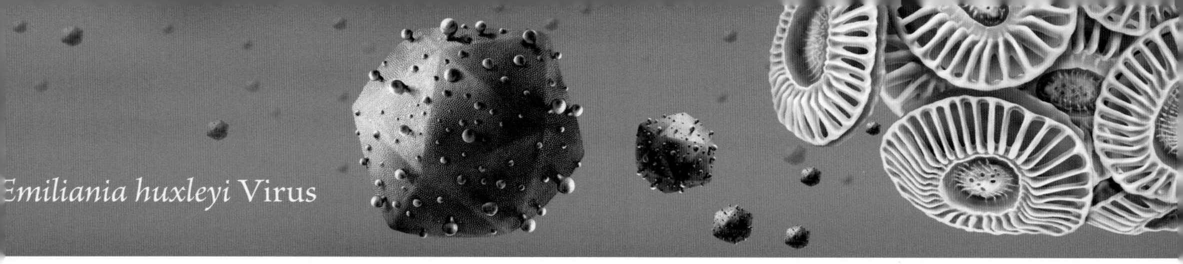

You may think viruses are just things that make people sick, but they play an important role in maintaining the ocean's natural balance. Without ocean viruses to keep them in check, algae would continue to grow until they exhausted their own food supply, starving themselves into extermination. Photosynthetic algae like *E. huxleyi* are responsible for half the carbon dioxide fixation and oxygen production on the planet. Without algae, life on Earth wouldn't be possible, for humans or anything else.

Viruses like EhV restore the balance during an *E. huxleyi* outbreak, a job only they can do. It's a delicate task—killing too many *E. huxleyi* could be as bad as killing too few. To prevent the virus from killing off too many algae, *E. huxleyi* has evolved an escape strategy. This marine alga is capable of transforming itself to a speedy, free-swimming form—sort of like an escape pod—ensuring that some *E. huxleyi* will survive.

Scientists are just beginning to understand the crucial role ocean viruses like EhV play in the global ecosystem, essential to the survival of life on Earth. By keeping algae in check and the oceans in balance, ocean viruses make it possible for us to go about our daily lives. It's a never-ending battle, but one that the viruses are winning, at least for now.

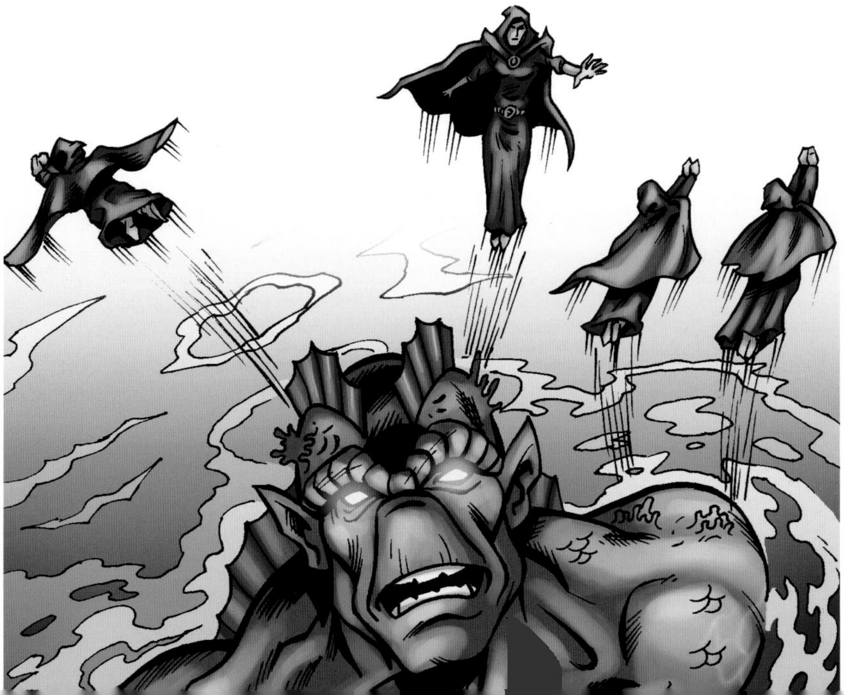

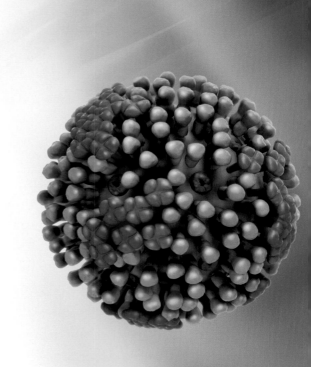

Influenza
VIRUS

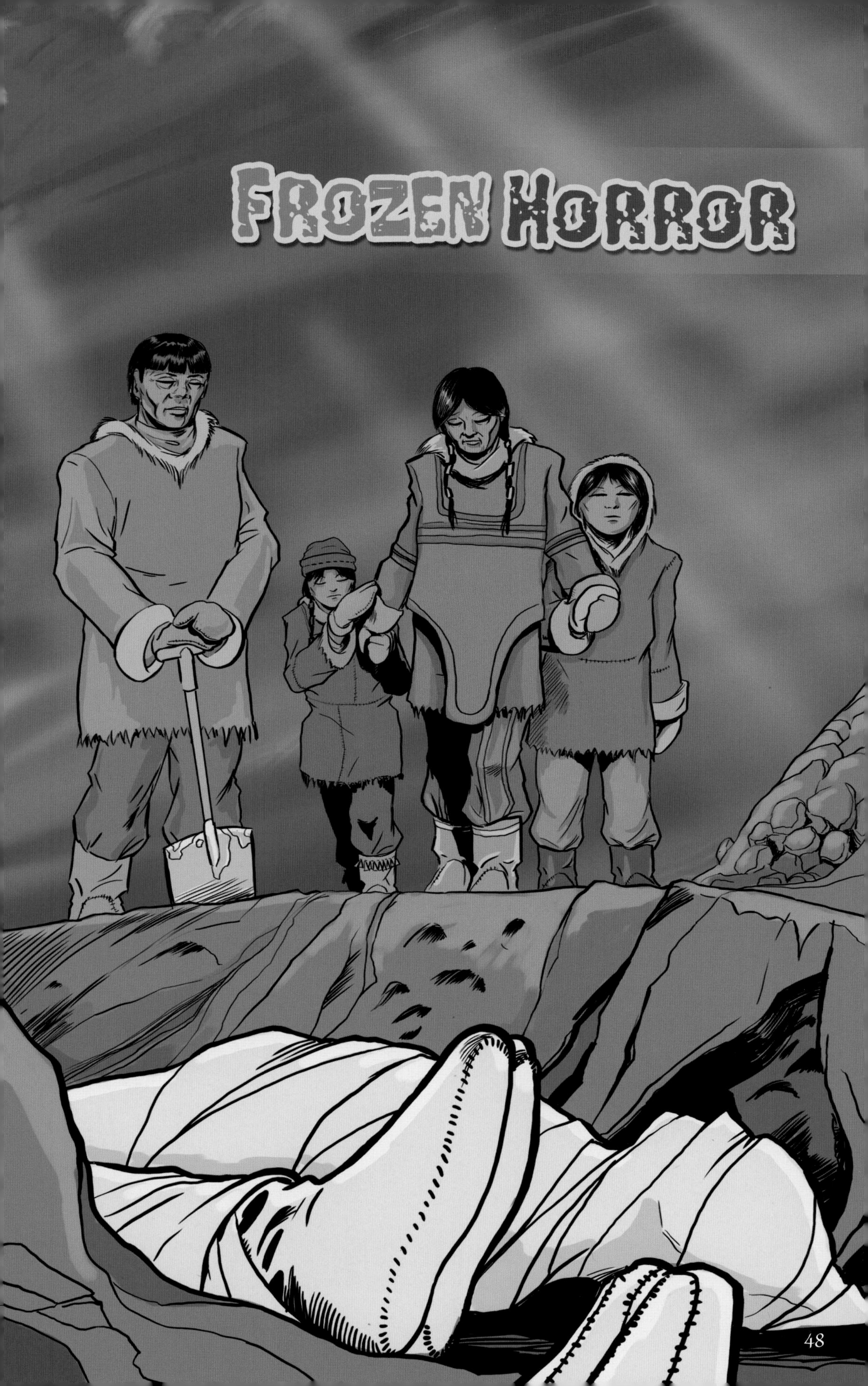
FROZEN HORROR

FROZEN HORROR

THIS IS THE PLACE. TRANSLATED BY THE NATIVES AS "*THE LAND OF HAUNTED SHADOWS*."

I CAN SEE WHY.

NOT FOUND ON ANY ALASKAN MAP, THE LOCATION IS KNOWN ONLY THROUGH WORD—OF—MOUTH, PASSED DOWN THROUGH COUNTLESS GENERATIONS.

TOOK ME THE BETTER PART OF A YEAR TO LOCATE IT.

SO, THIS IS WHAT *IT* LOOKS LIKE.

SO QUIET AND SERENE. NO ONE WOULD EVER THINK THIS WAS ONCE THE SITE OF A *MASSACRE*...

...AND ONE OF THE GREATEST *BIOLOGICAL MYSTERIES* ON THE PLANET.

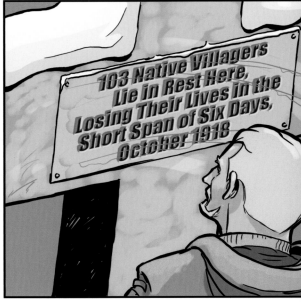

103 Native Villagers Lie in Rest Here, Losing Their Lives in the Short Span of Six Days, October 1918

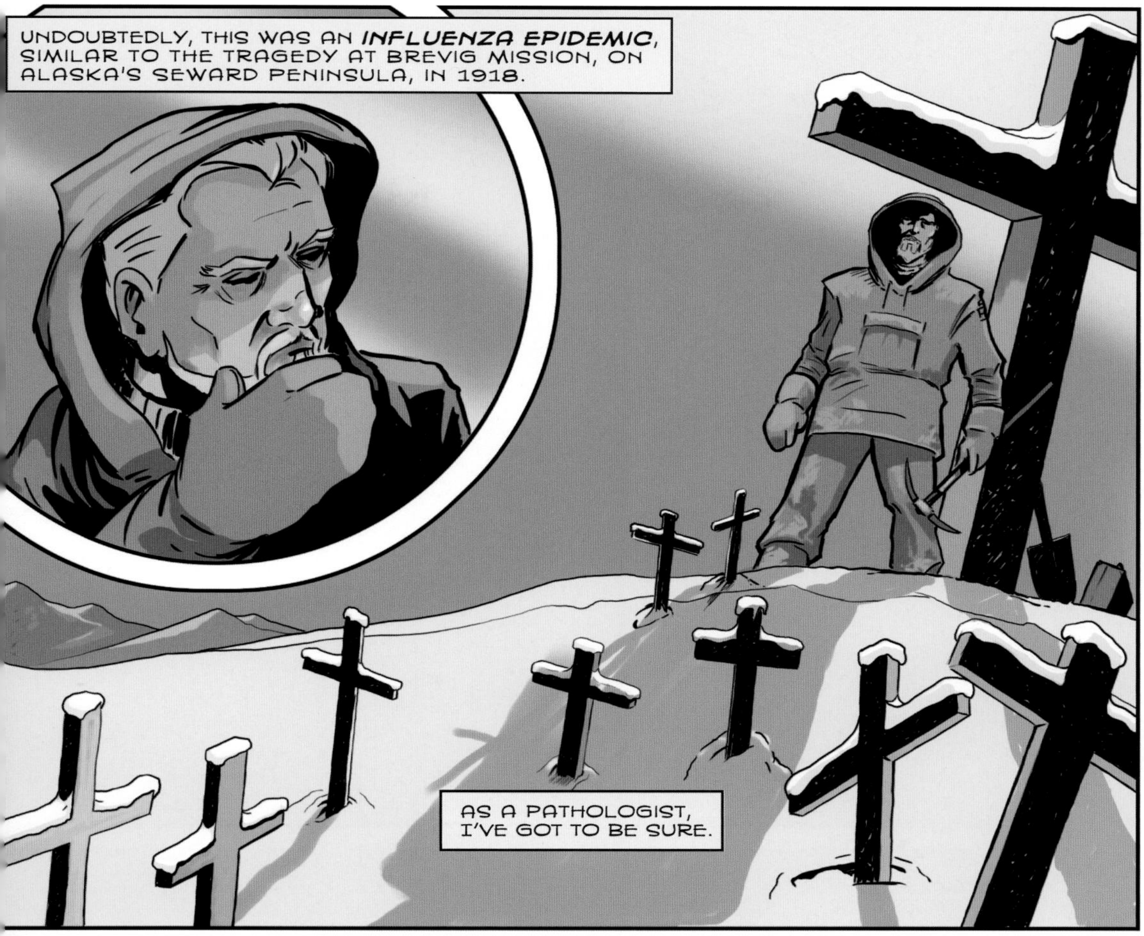
UNDOUBTEDLY, THIS WAS AN *INFLUENZA EPIDEMIC*, SIMILAR TO THE TRAGEDY AT BREVIG MISSION, ON ALASKA'S SEWARD PENINSULA, IN 1918.
AS A PATHOLOGIST, I'VE GOT TO BE SURE.

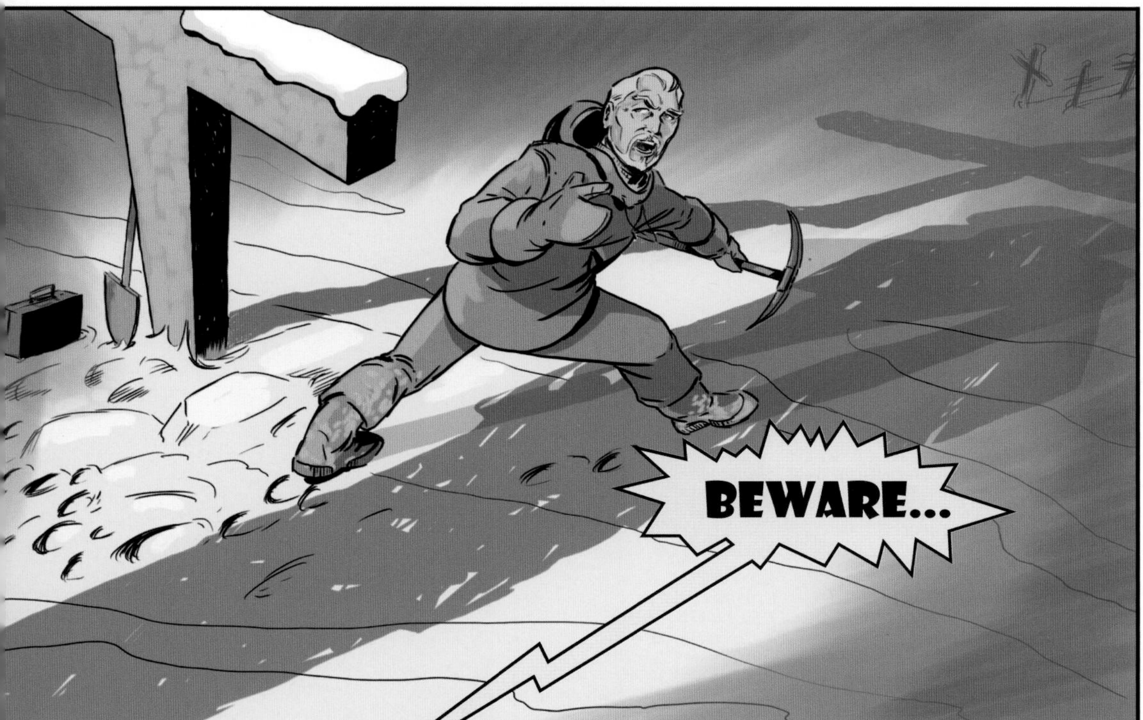
BEWARE...

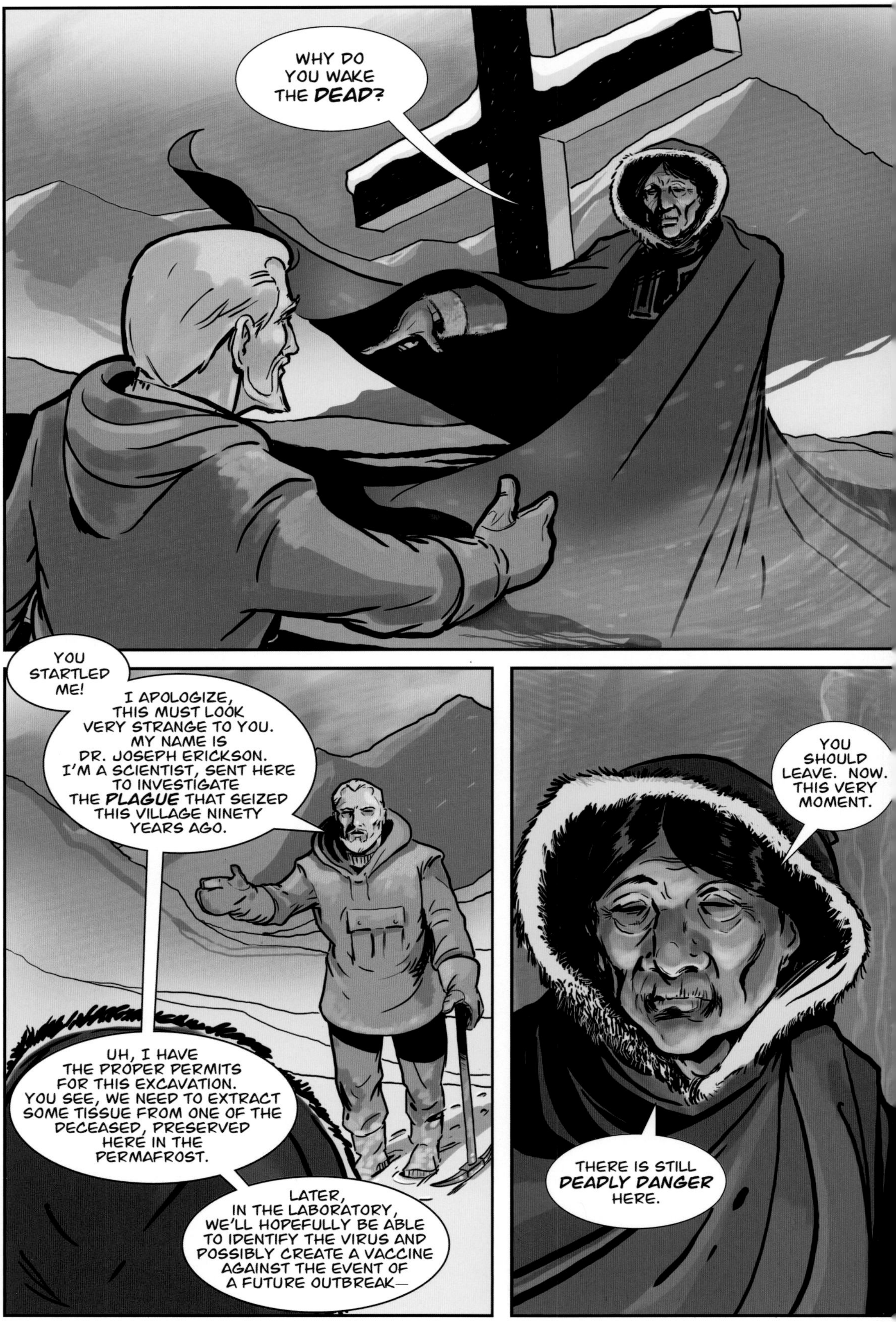
WHY DO YOU WAKE THE DEAD?
YOU STARTLED ME!
I APOLOGIZE, THIS MUST LOOK VERY STRANGE TO YOU. MY NAME IS DR. JOSEPH ERICKSON. I'M A SCIENTIST, SENT HERE TO INVESTIGATE THE PLAGUE THAT SEIZED THIS VILLAGE NINETY YEARS AGO.
UH, I HAVE THE PROPER PERMITS FOR THIS EXCAVATION. YOU SEE, WE NEED TO EXTRACT SOME TISSUE FROM ONE OF THE DECEASED, PRESERVED HERE IN THE PERMAFROST.
LATER, IN THE LABORATORY, WE'LL HOPEFULLY BE ABLE TO IDENTIFY THE VIRUS AND POSSIBLY CREATE A VACCINE AGAINST THE EVENT OF A FUTURE OUTBREAK—
YOU SHOULD LEAVE. NOW. THIS VERY MOMENT.
THERE IS STILL DEADLY DANGER HERE.

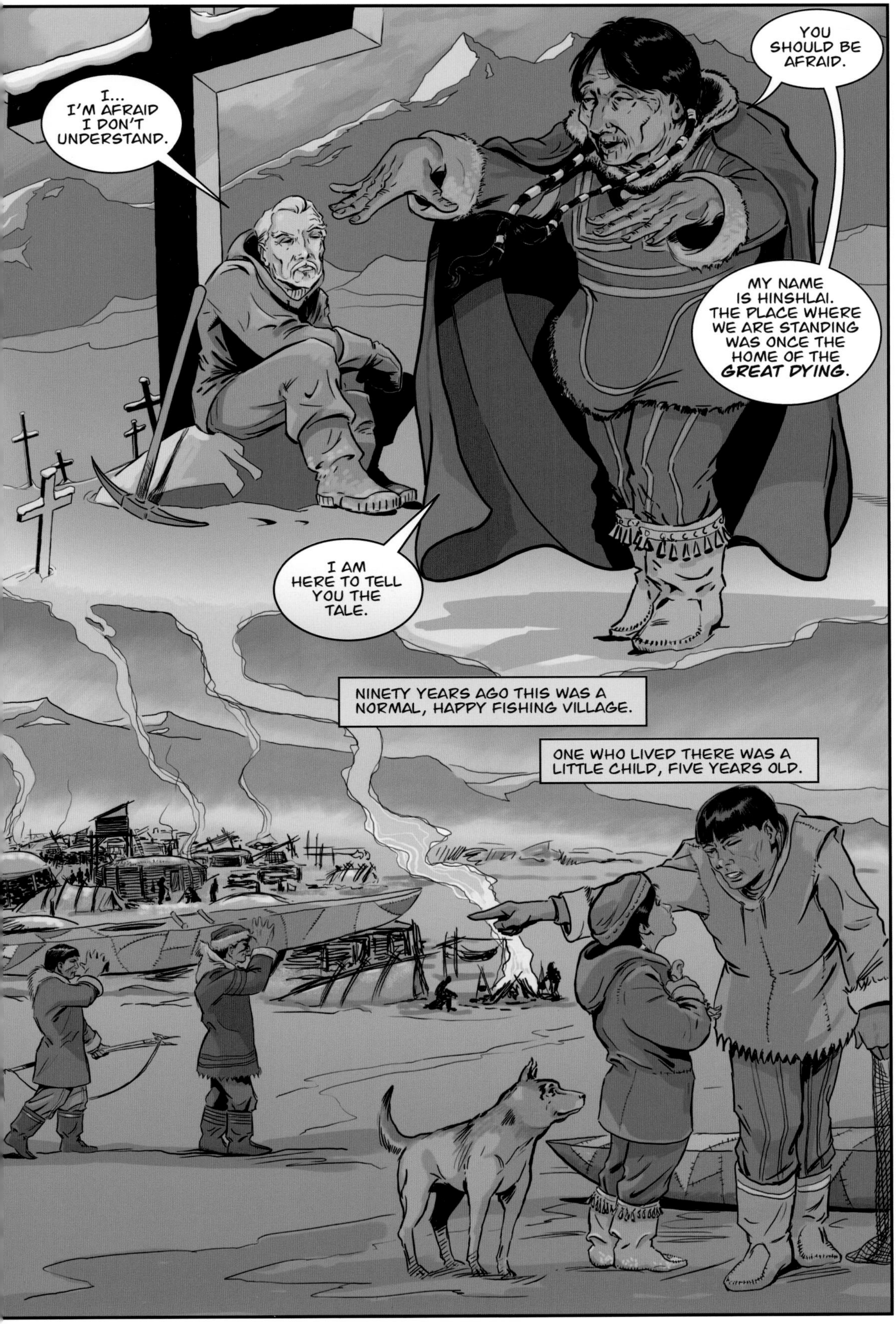
I... I'M AFRAID I DON'T UNDERSTAND.
YOU SHOULD BE AFRAID.
MY NAME IS HINSHLAI. THE PLACE WHERE WE ARE STANDING WAS ONCE THE HOME OF THE GREAT DYING.
I AM HERE TO TELL YOU THE TALE.
NINETY YEARS AGO THIS WAS A NORMAL, HAPPY FISHING VILLAGE.
ONE WHO LIVED THERE WAS A LITTLE CHILD, FIVE YEARS OLD.

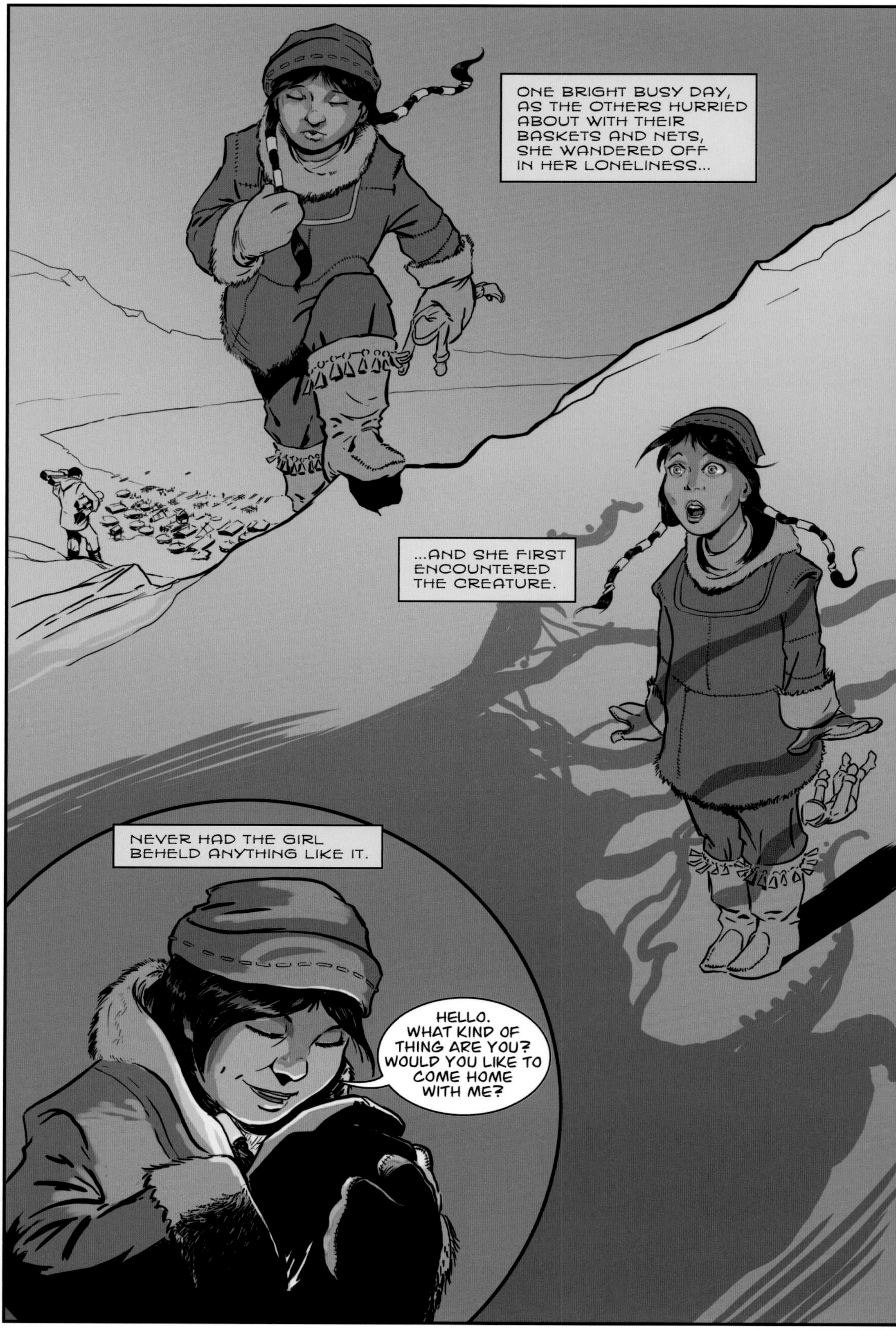
ONE BRIGHT BUSY DAY, AS THE OTHERS HURRIED ABOUT WITH THEIR BASKETS AND NETS, SHE WANDERED OFF IN HER LONELINESS...
...AND SHE FIRST ENCOUNTERED THE CREATURE.
NEVER HAD THE GIRL BEHELD ANYTHING LIKE IT.
HELLO. WHAT KIND OF THING ARE YOU? WOULD YOU LIKE TO COME HOME WITH ME?

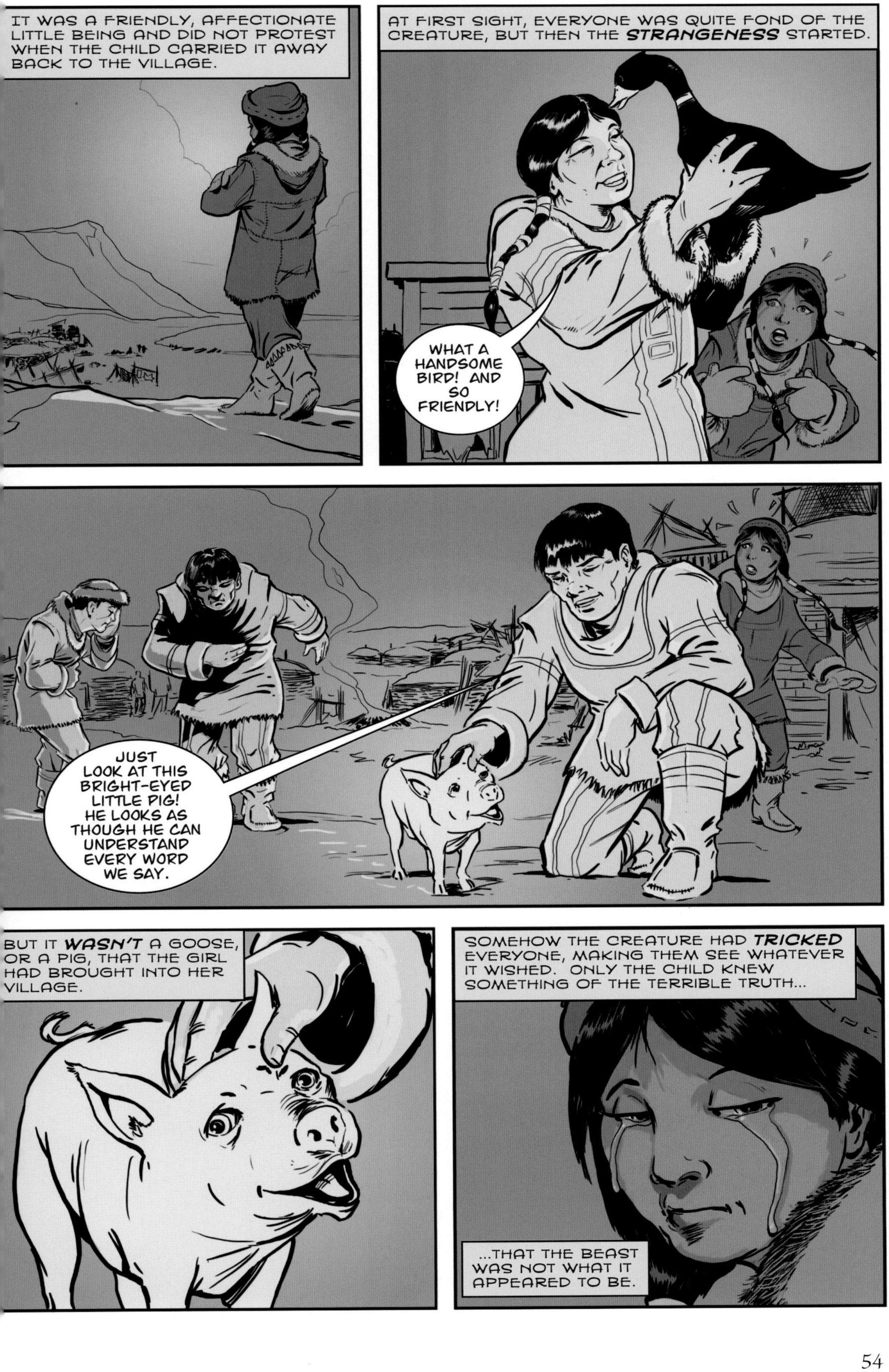
IT WAS A FRIENDLY, AFFECTIONATE LITTLE BEING AND DID NOT PROTEST WHEN THE CHILD CARRIED IT AWAY BACK TO THE VILLAGE.
AT FIRST SIGHT, EVERYONE WAS QUITE FOND OF THE CREATURE, BUT THEN THE STRANGENESS STARTED.
WHAT A HANDSOME BIRD! AND SO FRIENDLY!
JUST LOOK AT THIS BRIGHT-EYED LITTLE PIG! HE LOOKS AS THOUGH HE CAN UNDERSTAND EVERY WORD WE SAY.
BUT IT WASN'T A GOOSE, OR A PIG, THAT THE GIRL HAD BROUGHT INTO HER VILLAGE.
SOMEHOW THE CREATURE HAD TRICKED EVERYONE, MAKING THEM SEE WHATEVER IT WISHED. ONLY THE CHILD KNEW SOMETHING OF THE TERRIBLE TRUTH...
...THAT THE BEAST WAS NOT WHAT IT APPEARED TO BE.

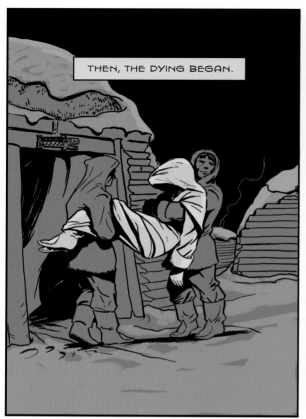

THEN, THE DYING BEGAN.

QUICK, CRUEL AND BRUTAL.

UNRELENTING.

NEARLY EVERYONE WAS AFFECTED.

MOTHER...? MOTHER, CAN YOU HEAR ME...?

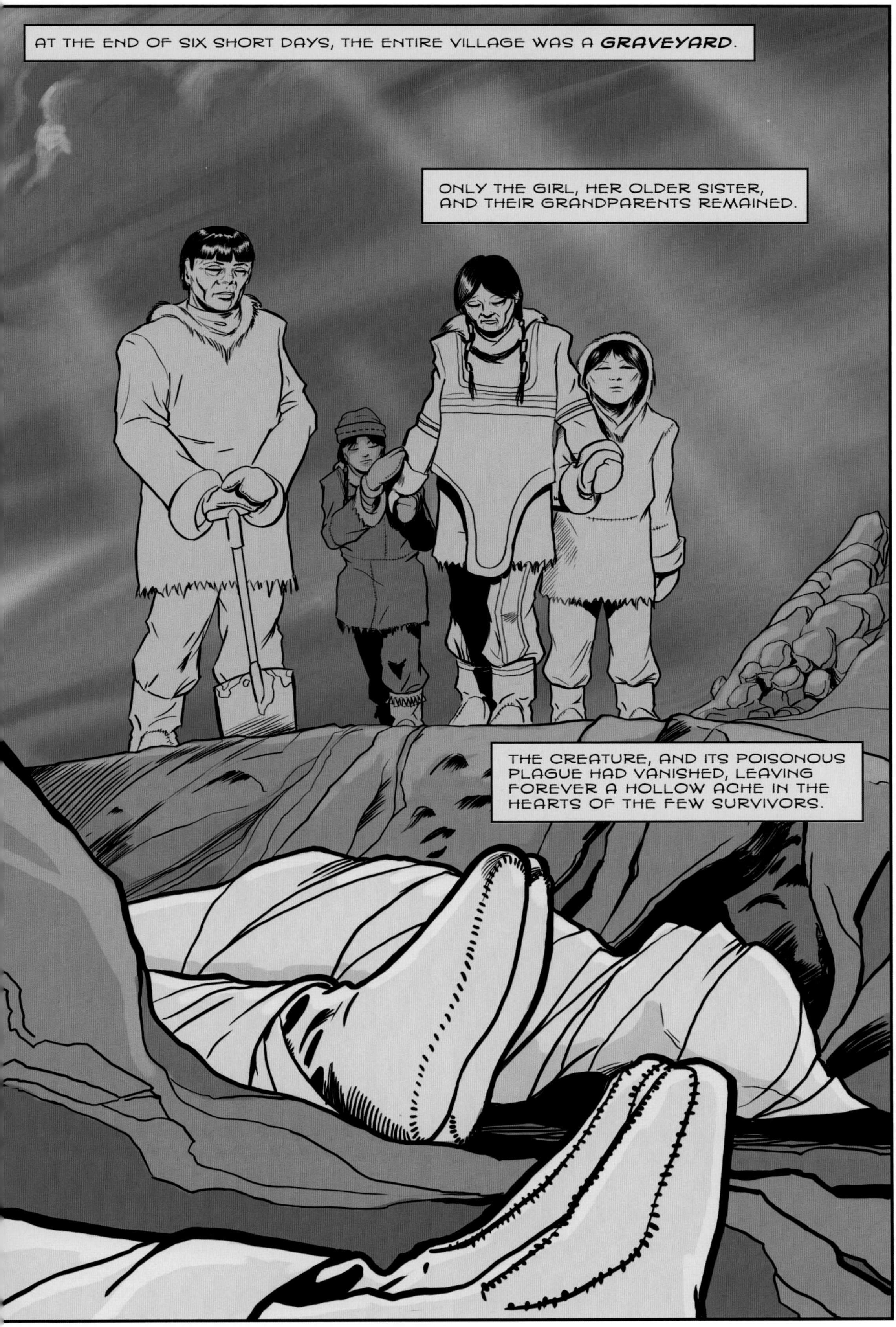
AT THE END OF SIX SHORT DAYS, THE ENTIRE VILLAGE WAS A GRAVEYARD.
ONLY THE GIRL, HER OLDER SISTER, AND THEIR GRANDPARENTS REMAINED.
THE CREATURE, AND ITS POISONOUS PLAGUE HAD VANISHED, LEAVING FOREVER A HOLLOW ACHE IN THE HEARTS OF THE FEW SURVIVORS.

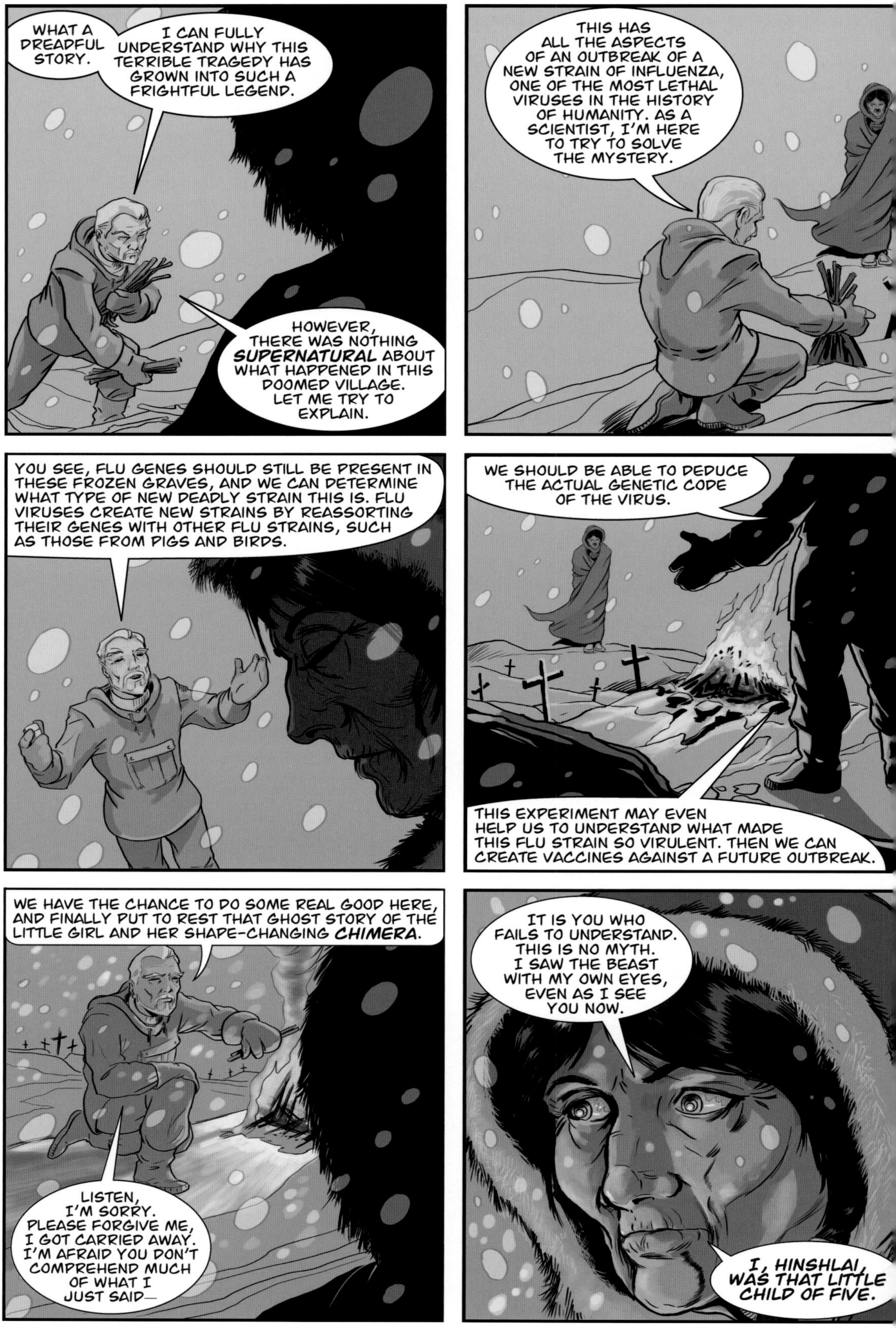
WHAT A DREADFUL STORY.
I CAN FULLY UNDERSTAND WHY THIS TERRIBLE TRAGEDY HAS GROWN INTO SUCH A FRIGHTFUL LEGEND.
HOWEVER, THERE WAS NOTHING SUPERNATURAL ABOUT WHAT HAPPENED IN THIS DOOMED VILLAGE. LET ME TRY TO EXPLAIN.
THIS HAS ALL THE ASPECTS OF AN OUTBREAK OF A NEW STRAIN OF INFLUENZA, ONE OF THE MOST LETHAL VIRUSES IN THE HISTORY OF HUMANITY. AS A SCIENTIST, I'M HERE TO TRY TO SOLVE THE MYSTERY.
YOU SEE, FLU GENES SHOULD STILL BE PRESENT IN THESE FROZEN GRAVES, AND WE CAN DETERMINE WHAT TYPE OF NEW DEADLY STRAIN THIS IS. FLU VIRUSES CREATE NEW STRAINS BY REASSORTING THEIR GENES WITH OTHER FLU STRAINS, SUCH AS THOSE FROM PIGS AND BIRDS.
WE SHOULD BE ABLE TO DEDUCE THE ACTUAL GENETIC CODE OF THE VIRUS.
THIS EXPERIMENT MAY EVEN HELP US TO UNDERSTAND WHAT MADE THIS FLU STRAIN SO VIRULENT. THEN WE CAN CREATE VACCINES AGAINST A FUTURE OUTBREAK.
WE HAVE THE CHANCE TO DO SOME REAL GOOD HERE, AND FINALLY PUT TO REST THAT GHOST STORY OF THE LITTLE GIRL AND HER SHAPE-CHANGING CHIMERA.
LISTEN, I'M SORRY. PLEASE FORGIVE ME, I GOT CARRIED AWAY. I'M AFRAID YOU DON'T COMPREHEND MUCH OF WHAT I JUST SAID—
IT IS YOU WHO FAILS TO UNDERSTAND. THIS IS NO MYTH. I SAW THE BEAST WITH MY OWN EYES, EVEN AS I SEE YOU NOW.
I, HINSHLAI, WAS THAT LITTLE CHILD OF FIVE.

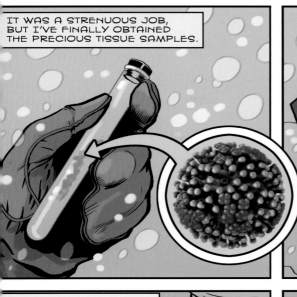

IT WAS A STRENUOUS JOB, BUT I'VE FINALLY OBTAINED THE PRECIOUS TISSUE SAMPLES.

A GROWING BLIZZARD IS ALREADY BEGINNING TO HOWL. I WON'T BE SORRY TO LEAVE THIS EERIE SITE FAR BEHIND ME.

THE OLD NATIVE WOMAN VANISHED DURING MY WORK. THE SNOW HAS COVERED HER TRACKS.

IT'S ALMOST AS IF SHE WAS NEVER HERE AT ALL.

SQUAWK

OH—! WELL, HELLO THERE. WHERE DID YOU COME FROM? I'M SURE YOU WEREN'T THERE A MINUTE AGO.

HMM, YOU'RE HURT. LOOKS LIKE A BROKEN WING. YOU'D NEVER SURVIVE OUT IN THIS STORM.

SO, I'LL TAKE YOU WITH ME.

WE HAVE A VETERINARIAN AT THE BASE. SHE'LL FIX YOU UP, GOOD AS NEW.

STRANGE, THOUGH. FOR A MOMENT, THERE IN THE SNOW, I COULD HAVE SWORN THAT YOU WERE A BABY PIG! HOW COULD I MAKE SUCH A MISTAKE?

THIS WEATHER SURE DOES WEIRD THINGS TO THE IMAGINATION.

BET EVERYONE WILL BE SURPRISED WHEN THEY SEE ME WALK IN WITH YOU.

END?

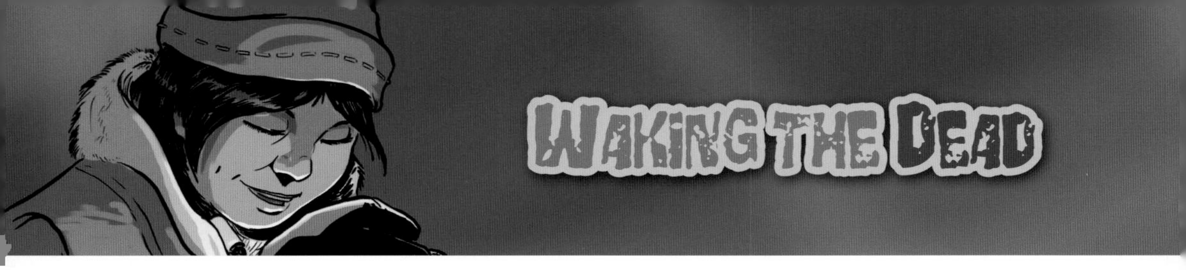

Waking the Dead

by Ann Downer-Hazell

In remote places in Alaska, scientists armed with permits and shovels are venturing out onto the frozen tundra. Their mission: to wake the ghosts sleeping in the permafrost.

It's a long drive by Jeep to a place like Brevig Misson, Alaska. It's also a journey back in time. Almost one hundred years ago, the world was in the grip of a flu pandemic. In remote outposts like Brevig Mission, whole villages were wiped out in a matter of days by the deadly scourge. In some places, a cross is the only memorial left of entire communities—every man, woman, and child wiped out by one of the most deadly pathogens the world has ever known.

Scientists want to know how the tiny influenza virus manages to wreak such havoc. Over the last five years, pathologists—scientists who study the cause and effect of disease—have journeyed to the Arctic, back to villages along Alaska's Seward Peninsula, where almost a century ago flu raged unchecked. By exhuming the bodies of the epidemic's victims, pathologists hope to find traces of the 1918 virus in the frozen tissues. If the frozen ground has preserved the virus and its secrets well, scientists can use samples of infected tissue to culture the virus back in the lab. Then, by reading the virus's genetic fingerprint, they hope to identify the strain responsible for the 1918 outbreak.

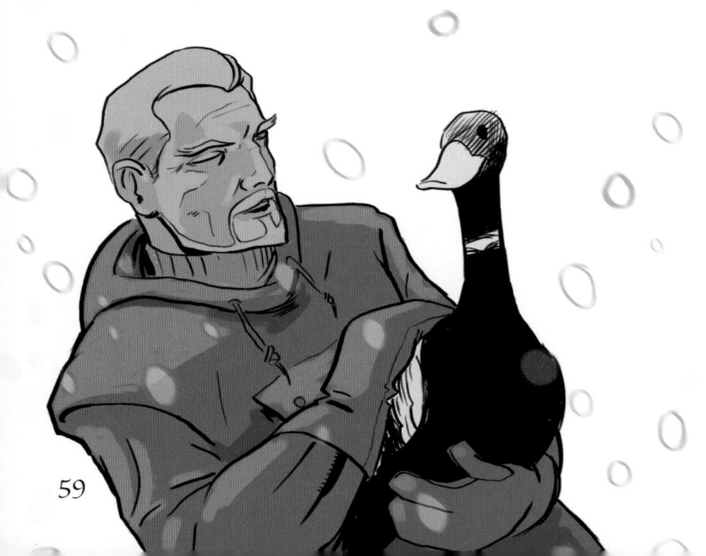

Influenza is a shape-shifter. Virologists think the strain of flu responsible for the 1918 pandemic may have started out in another species—influenza lives happily in other animals, including pigs and birds. When people first domesticated ducks, chickens, geese, and pigs, they began to live alongside them,

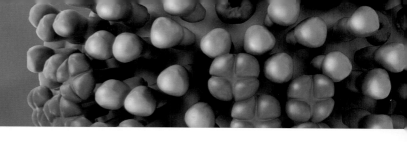

giving the viral shape-shifter a chance to mingle and adapt. New strains of flu arise when the virus has a chance to exchange genes with other viruses already at home in an animal host in a process called reassortment. Some time before the 1918 outbreak, the influenza virus acquired the genes it needed to shape-shift and jump from its animal host to a new, human one.

In a remote Alaskan village in 1918, the flu would have spread quickly. Death would have been quick, cruel, and brutal, leaving few survivors to bury the dead and tell how the disaster had unfolded. Today researchers are looking to the dead to tell the story of this flu mystery. By analyzing frozen tissue samples from the 1918 victims, researchers hope to crack the virus's genetic code and understand what made the 1918 strain so very deadly. They hope to use that knowledge to design a more effective vaccine to protect against a future outbreak.

To the ancient Greeks, a chimera was a fantastic monster, part lion, part snake, part goat. To scientists, influenza is a different kind of chimera—part virus, part pig, part bird. Will flu stay one step ahead of us, ever changing? Who will write the last chapter in this frozen medical mystery?

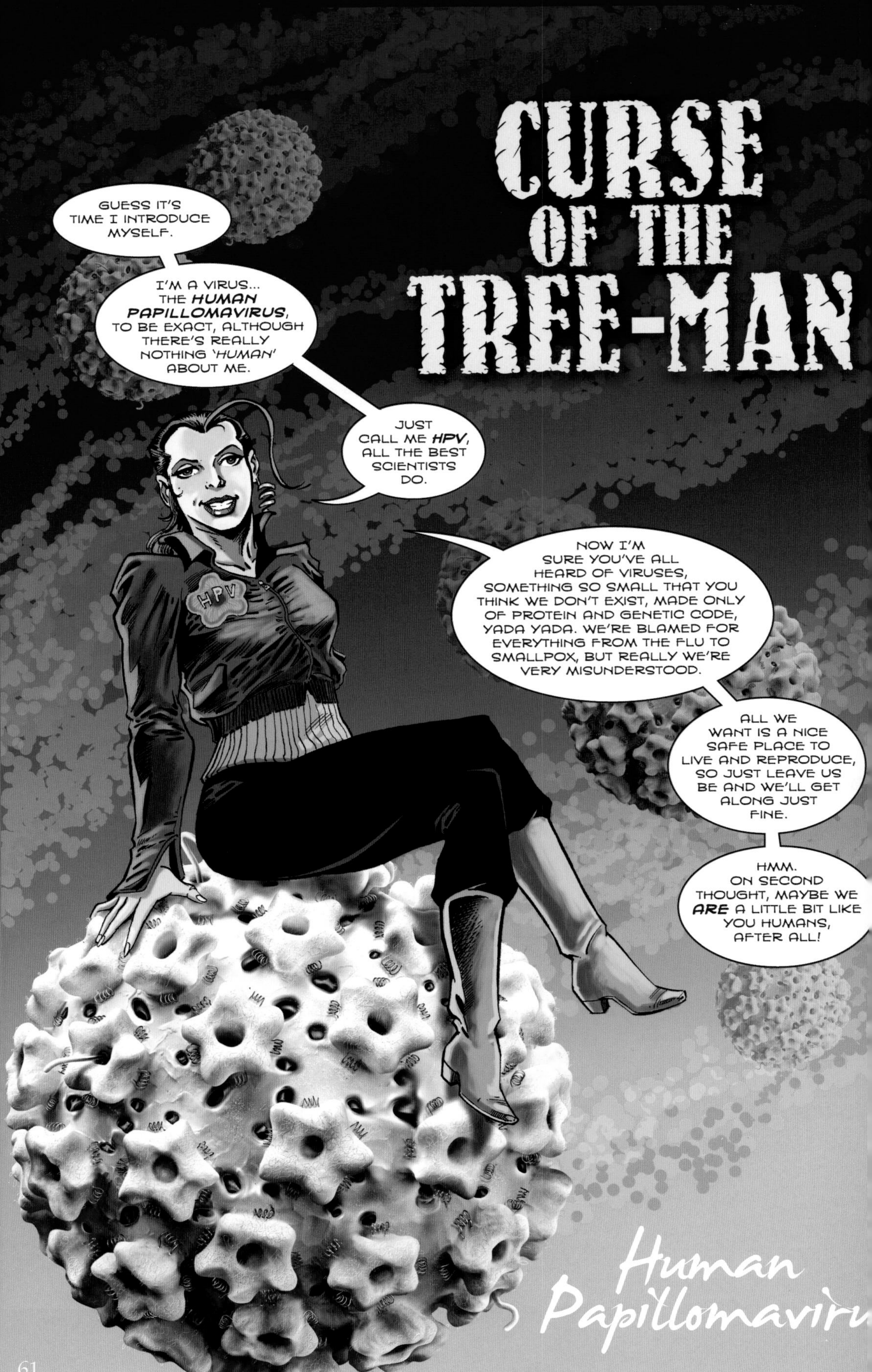
CURSE OF THE TREE-MAN
GUESS IT'S TIME I INTRODUCE MYSELF.
I'M A VIRUS... THE HUMAN PAPILLOMAVIRUS, TO BE EXACT, ALTHOUGH THERE'S REALLY NOTHING 'HUMAN' ABOUT ME.
JUST CALL ME HPV, ALL THE BEST SCIENTISTS DO.
HPV
NOW I'M SURE YOU'VE ALL HEARD OF VIRUSES, SOMETHING SO SMALL THAT YOU THINK WE DON'T EXIST, MADE ONLY OF PROTEIN AND GENETIC CODE, YADA YADA. WE'RE BLAMED FOR EVERYTHING FROM THE FLU TO SMALLPOX, BUT REALLY WE'RE VERY MISUNDERSTOOD.
ALL WE WANT IS A NICE SAFE PLACE TO LIVE AND REPRODUCE, SO JUST LEAVE US BE AND WE'LL GET ALONG JUST FINE.
HMM. ON SECOND THOUGHT, MAYBE WE ARE A LITTLE BIT LIKE YOU HUMANS, AFTER ALL!
Human Papillomaviru

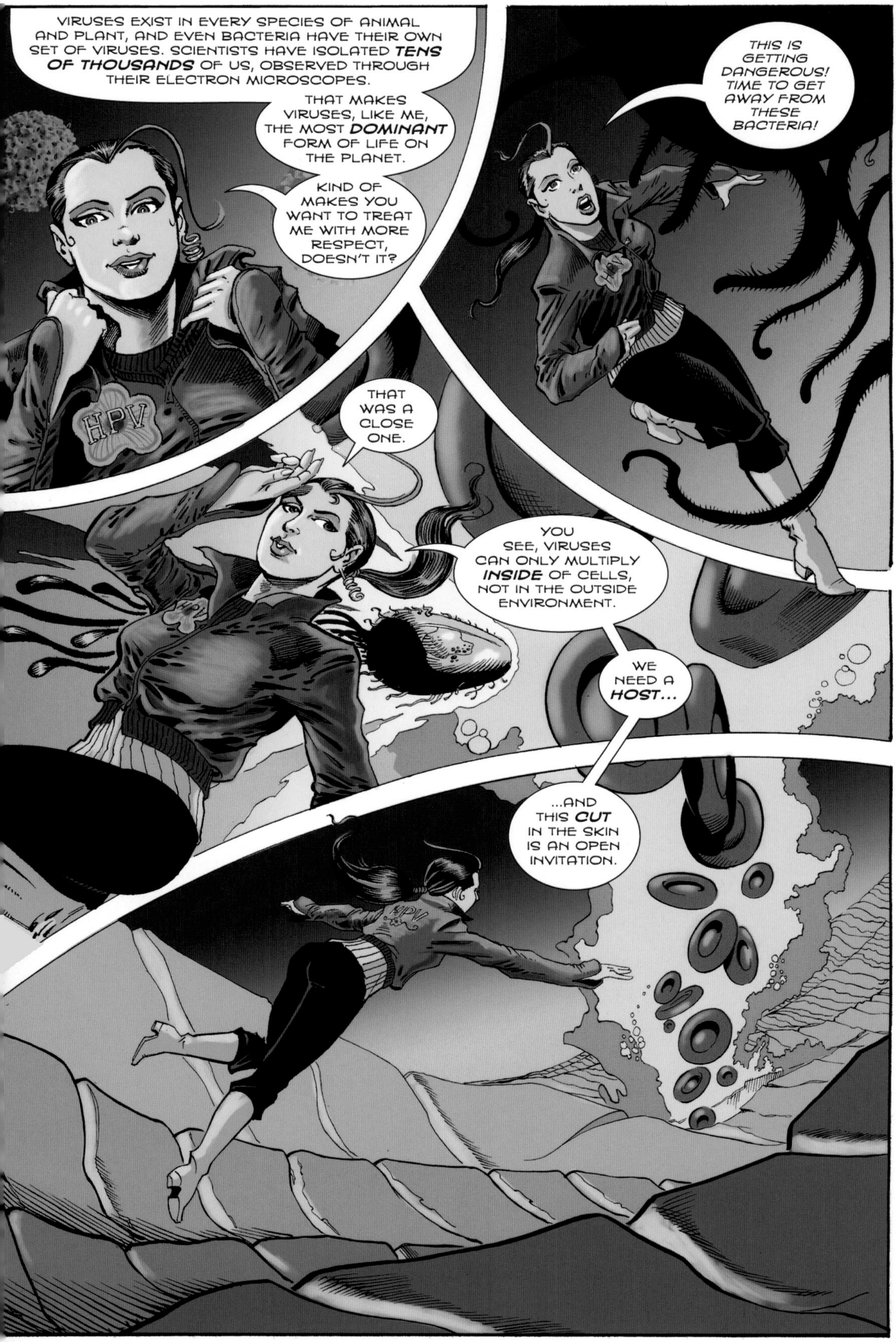
VIRUSES EXIST IN EVERY SPECIES OF ANIMAL AND PLANT, AND EVEN BACTERIA HAVE THEIR OWN SET OF VIRUSES. SCIENTISTS HAVE ISOLATED TENS OF THOUSANDS OF US, OBSERVED THROUGH THEIR ELECTRON MICROSCOPES.
THAT MAKES VIRUSES, LIKE ME, THE MOST DOMINANT FORM OF LIFE ON THE PLANET.
KIND OF MAKES YOU WANT TO TREAT ME WITH MORE RESPECT, DOESN'T IT?
HPV
THIS IS GETTING DANGEROUS! TIME TO GET AWAY FROM THESE BACTERIA!
THAT WAS A CLOSE ONE.
YOU SEE, VIRUSES CAN ONLY MULTIPLY INSIDE OF CELLS, NOT IN THE OUTSIDE ENVIRONMENT.
WE NEED A HOST...
...AND THIS CUT IN THE SKIN IS AN OPEN INVITATION.

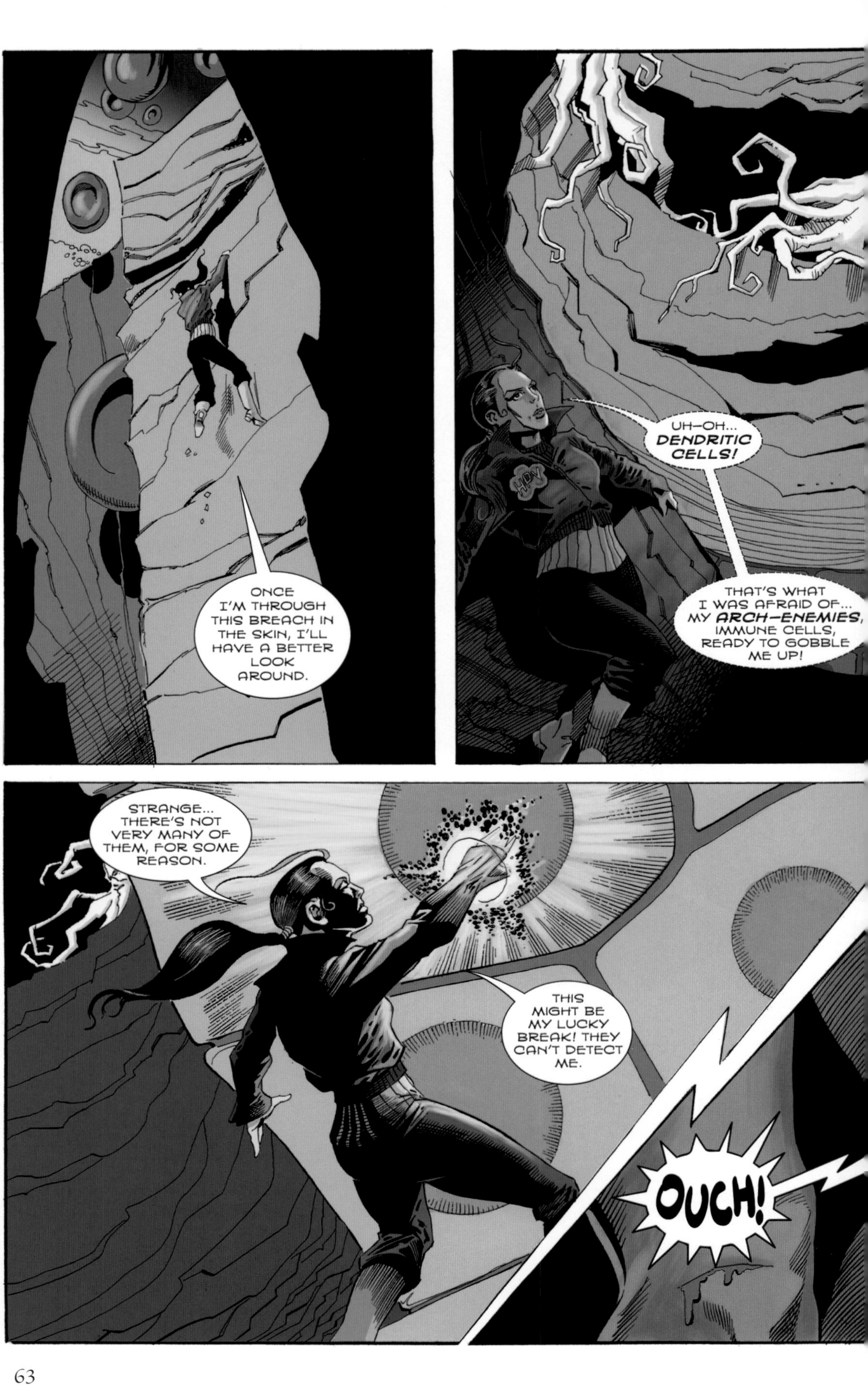
ONCE I'M THROUGH THIS BREACH IN THE SKIN, I'LL HAVE A BETTER LOOK AROUND.
UH-OH... DENDRITIC CELLS!
THAT'S WHAT I WAS AFRAID OF... MY ARCH-ENEMIES, IMMUNE CELLS, READY TO GOBBLE ME UP!
STRANGE... THERE'S NOT VERY MANY OF THEM, FOR SOME REASON.
THIS MIGHT BE MY LUCKY BREAK! THEY CAN'T DETECT ME.
OUCH!

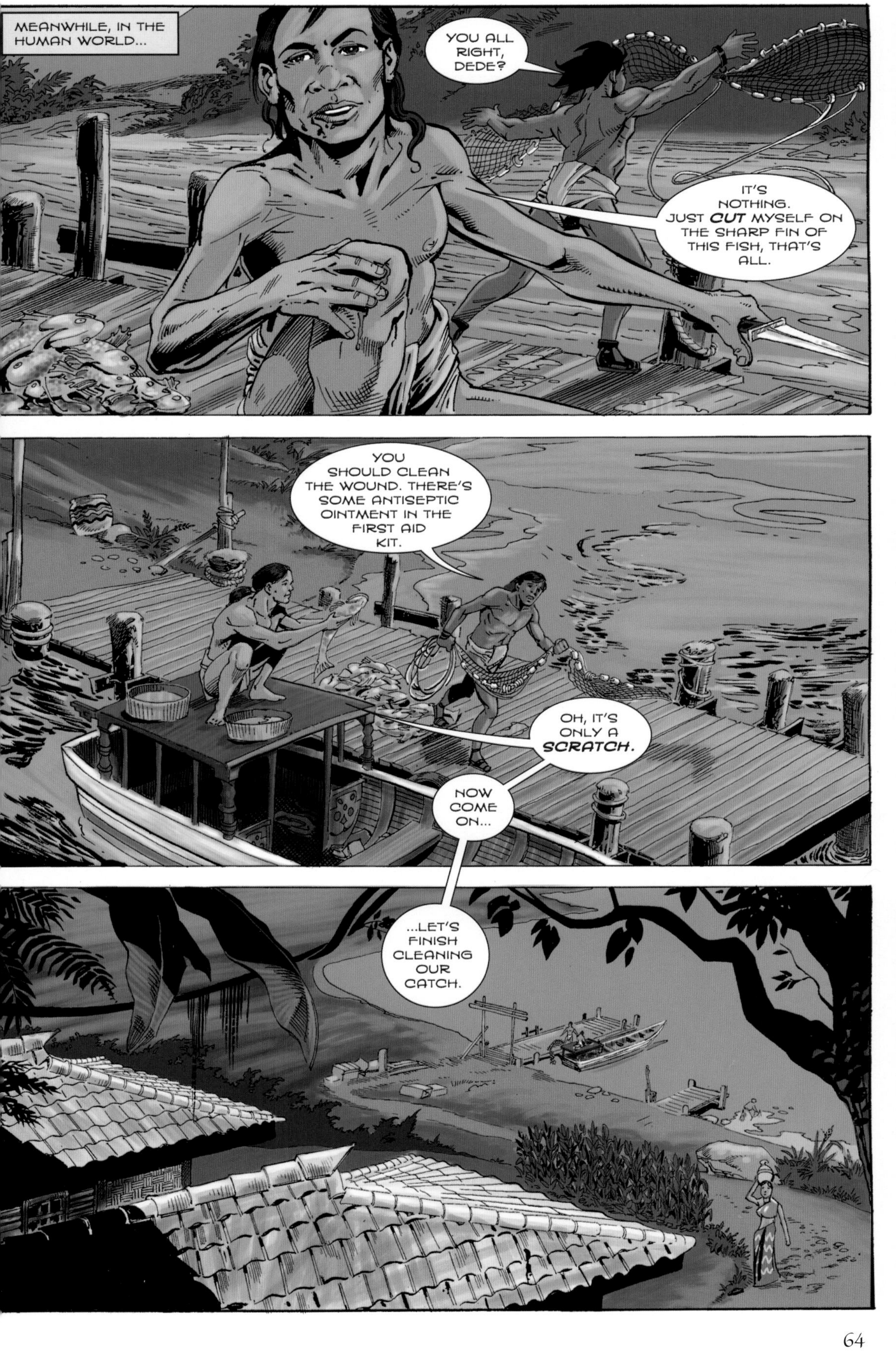
MEANWHILE, IN THE HUMAN WORLD...
YOU ALL RIGHT, DEDE?
IT'S NOTHING. JUST CUT MYSELF ON THE SHARP FIN OF THIS FISH, THAT'S ALL.
YOU SHOULD CLEAN THE WOUND. THERE'S SOME ANTISEPTIC OINTMENT IN THE FIRST AID KIT.
OH, IT'S ONLY A SCRATCH.
NOW COME ON...
...LET'S FINISH CLEANING OUR CATCH.

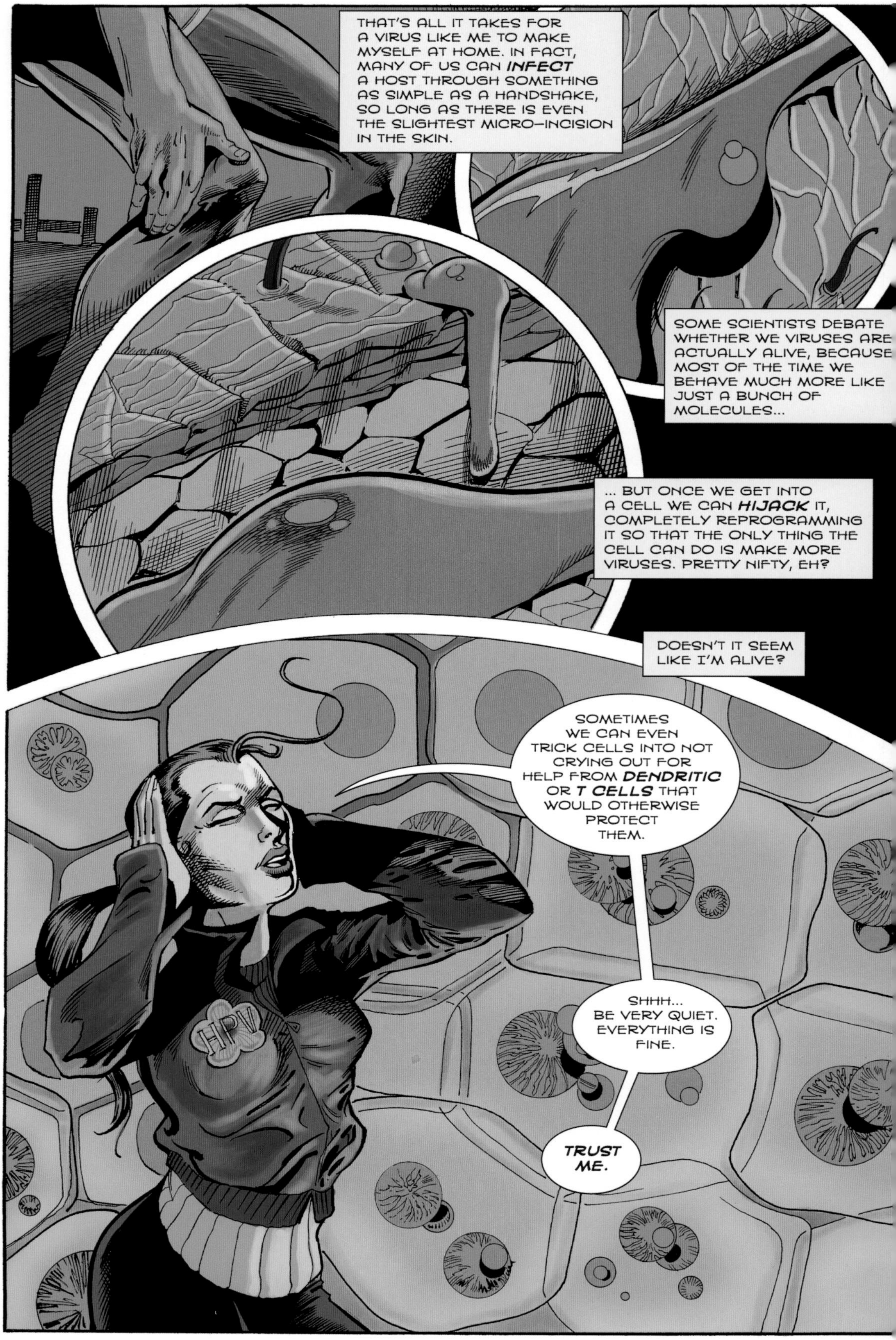
THAT'S ALL IT TAKES FOR A VIRUS LIKE ME TO MAKE MYSELF AT HOME. IN FACT, MANY OF US CAN *INFECT* A HOST THROUGH SOMETHING AS SIMPLE AS A HANDSHAKE, SO LONG AS THERE IS EVEN THE SLIGHTEST MICRO-INCISION IN THE SKIN.
SOME SCIENTISTS DEBATE WHETHER WE VIRUSES ARE ACTUALLY ALIVE, BECAUSE MOST OF THE TIME WE BEHAVE MUCH MORE LIKE JUST A BUNCH OF MOLECULES...
... BUT ONCE WE GET INTO A CELL WE CAN *HIJACK* IT, COMPLETELY REPROGRAMMING IT SO THAT THE ONLY THING THE CELL CAN DO IS MAKE MORE VIRUSES. PRETTY NIFTY, EH?
DOESN'T IT SEEM LIKE I'M ALIVE?
SOMETIMES WE CAN EVEN TRICK CELLS INTO NOT CRYING OUT FOR HELP FROM *DENDRITIC* OR *T CELLS* THAT WOULD OTHERWISE PROTECT THEM.
SHHH... BE VERY QUIET. EVERYTHING IS FINE.
TRUST ME.
HPV

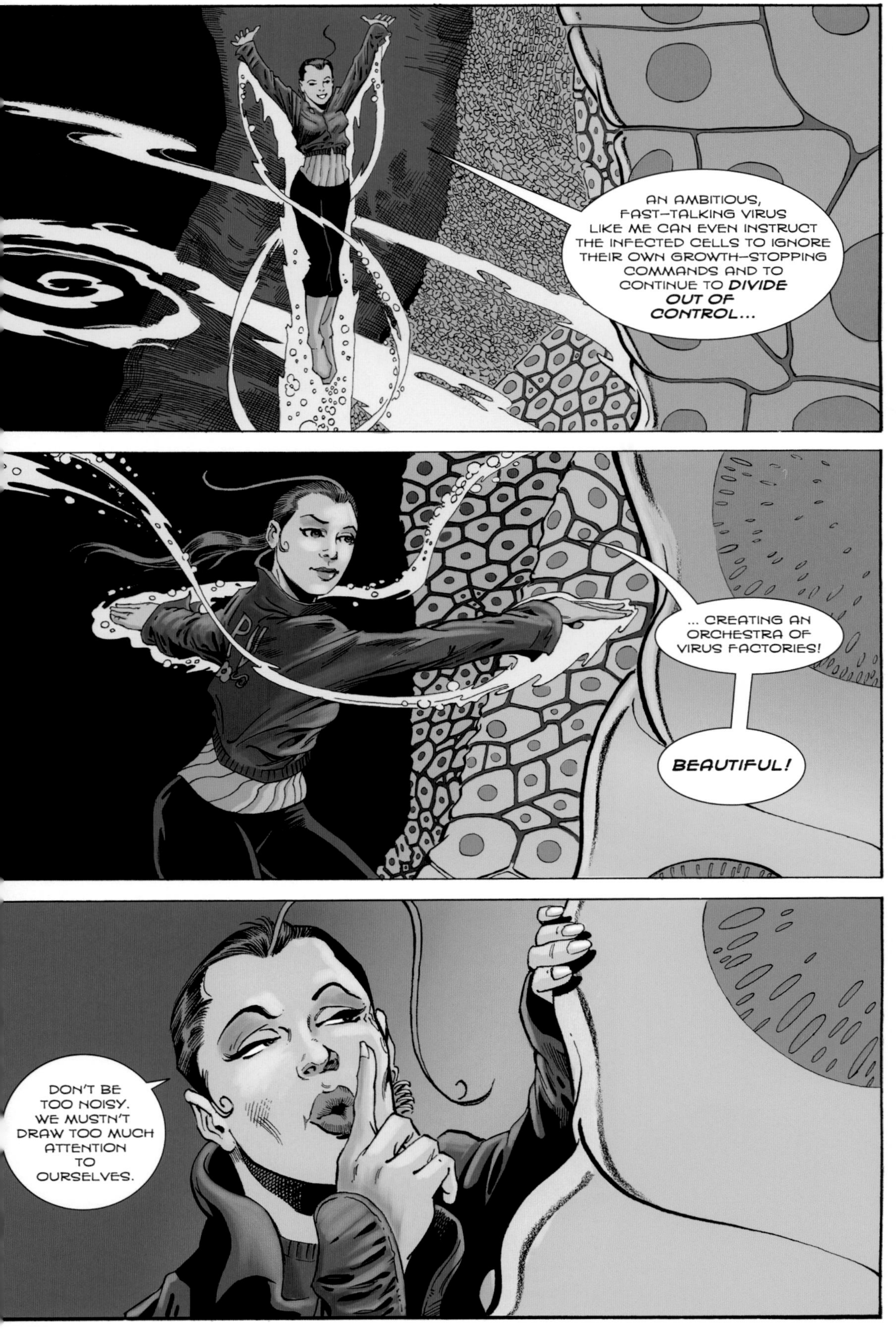
AN AMBITIOUS, FAST-TALKING VIRUS LIKE ME CAN EVEN INSTRUCT THE INFECTED CELLS TO IGNORE THEIR OWN GROWTH-STOPPING COMMANDS AND TO CONTINUE TO DIVIDE OUT OF CONTROL...
... CREATING AN ORCHESTRA OF VIRUS FACTORIES!
BEAUTIFUL!
DON'T BE TOO NOISY. WE MUSTN'T DRAW TOO MUCH ATTENTION TO OURSELVES.

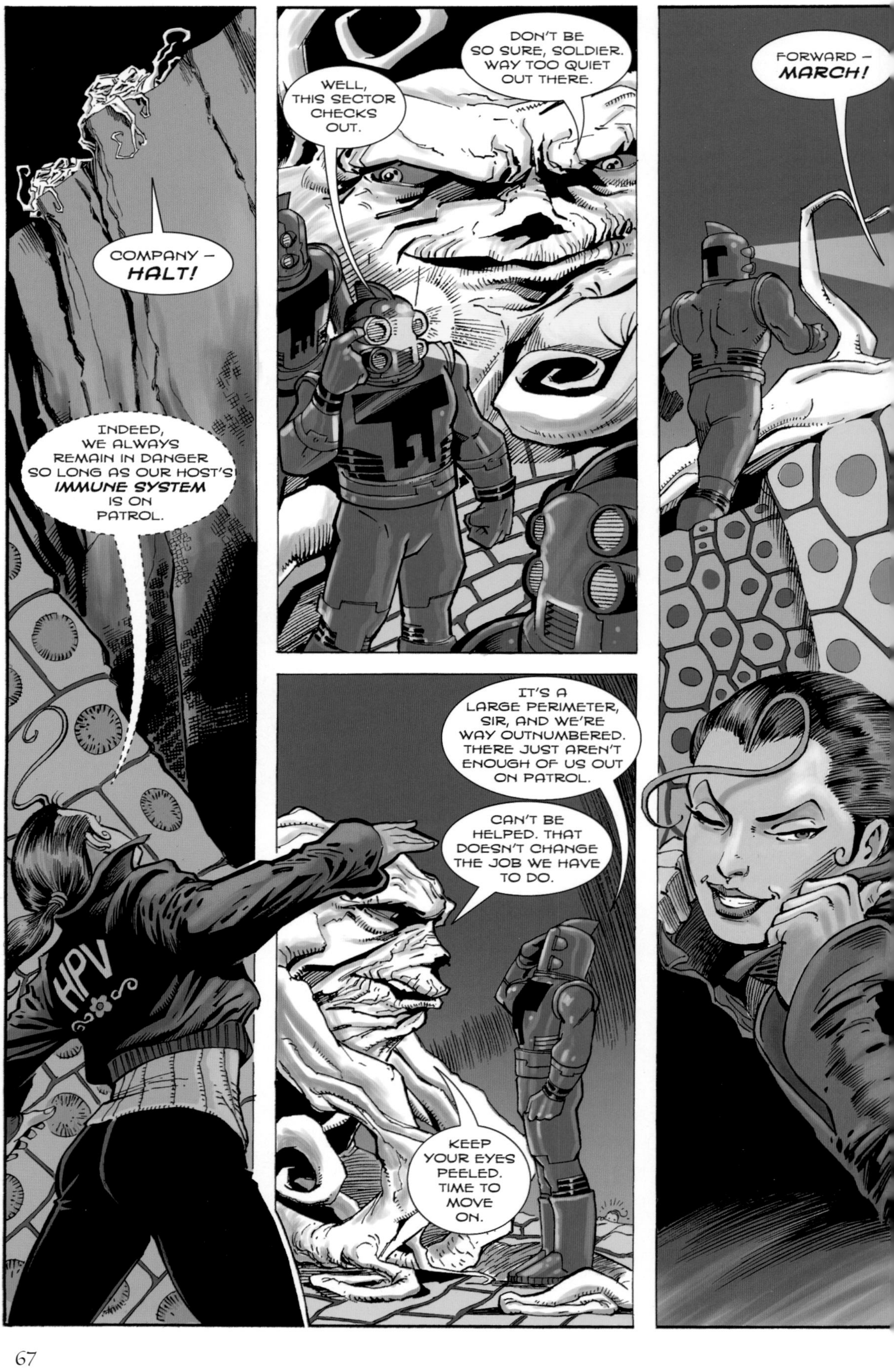
COMPANY — HALT!
INDEED, WE ALWAYS REMAIN IN DANGER SO LONG AS OUR HOST'S IMMUNE SYSTEM IS ON PATROL.
WELL, THIS SECTOR CHECKS OUT.
DON'T BE SO SURE, SOLDIER. WAY TOO QUIET OUT THERE.
IT'S A LARGE PERIMETER, SIR, AND WE'RE WAY OUTNUMBERED. THERE JUST AREN'T ENOUGH OF US OUT ON PATROL.
CAN'T BE HELPED. THAT DOESN'T CHANGE THE JOB WE HAVE TO DO.
KEEP YOUR EYES PEELED. TIME TO MOVE ON.
FORWARD — MARCH!
HPV

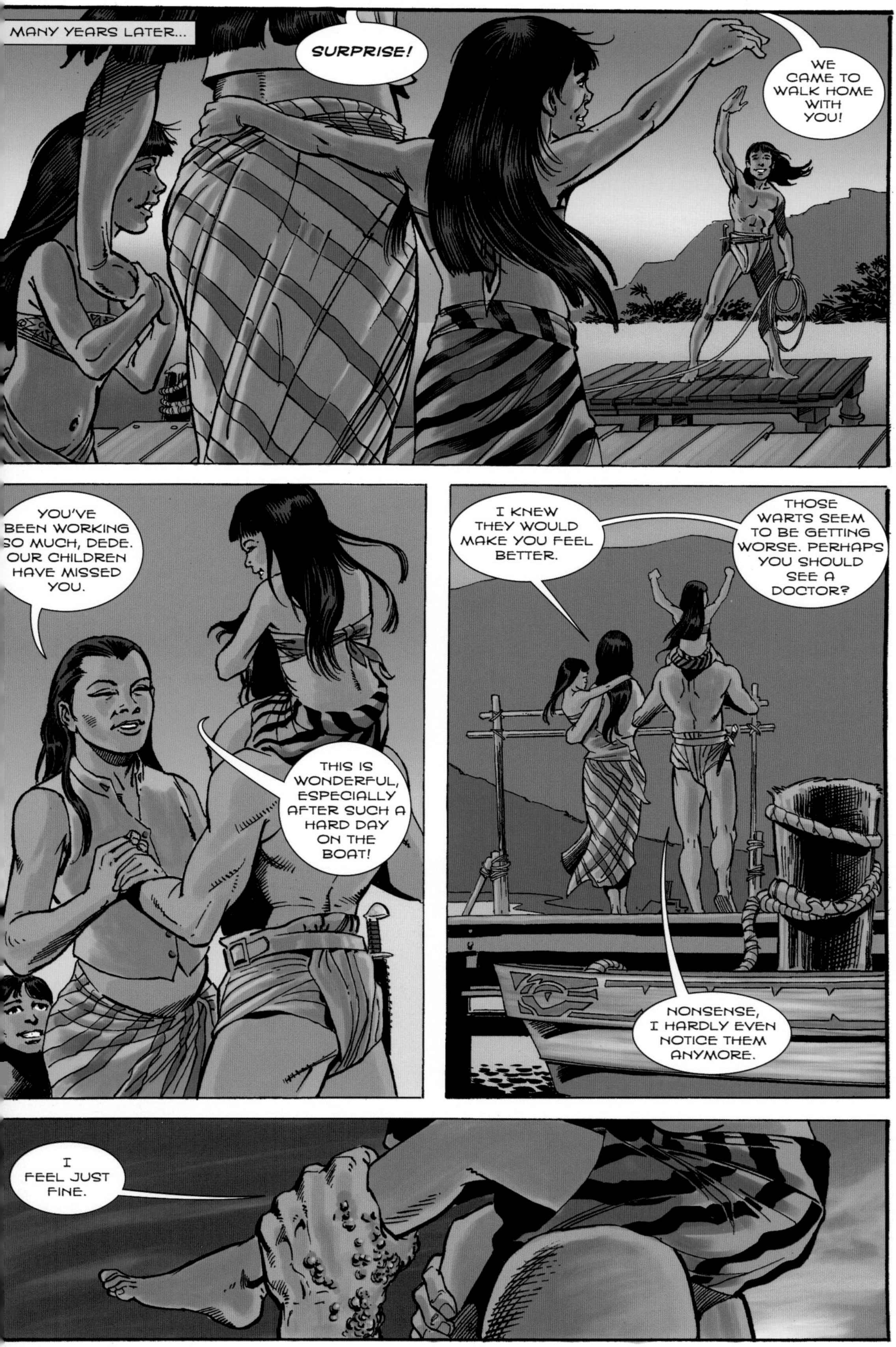
MANY YEARS LATER...
SURPRISE!
WE CAME TO WALK HOME WITH YOU!
YOU'VE BEEN WORKING SO MUCH, DEDE. OUR CHILDREN HAVE MISSED YOU.
THIS IS WONDERFUL, ESPECIALLY AFTER SUCH A HARD DAY ON THE BOAT!
I KNEW THEY WOULD MAKE YOU FEEL BETTER.
THOSE WARTS SEEM TO BE GETTING WORSE. PERHAPS YOU SHOULD SEE A DOCTOR?
NONSENSE, I HARDLY EVEN NOTICE THEM ANYMORE.
I FEEL JUST FINE.

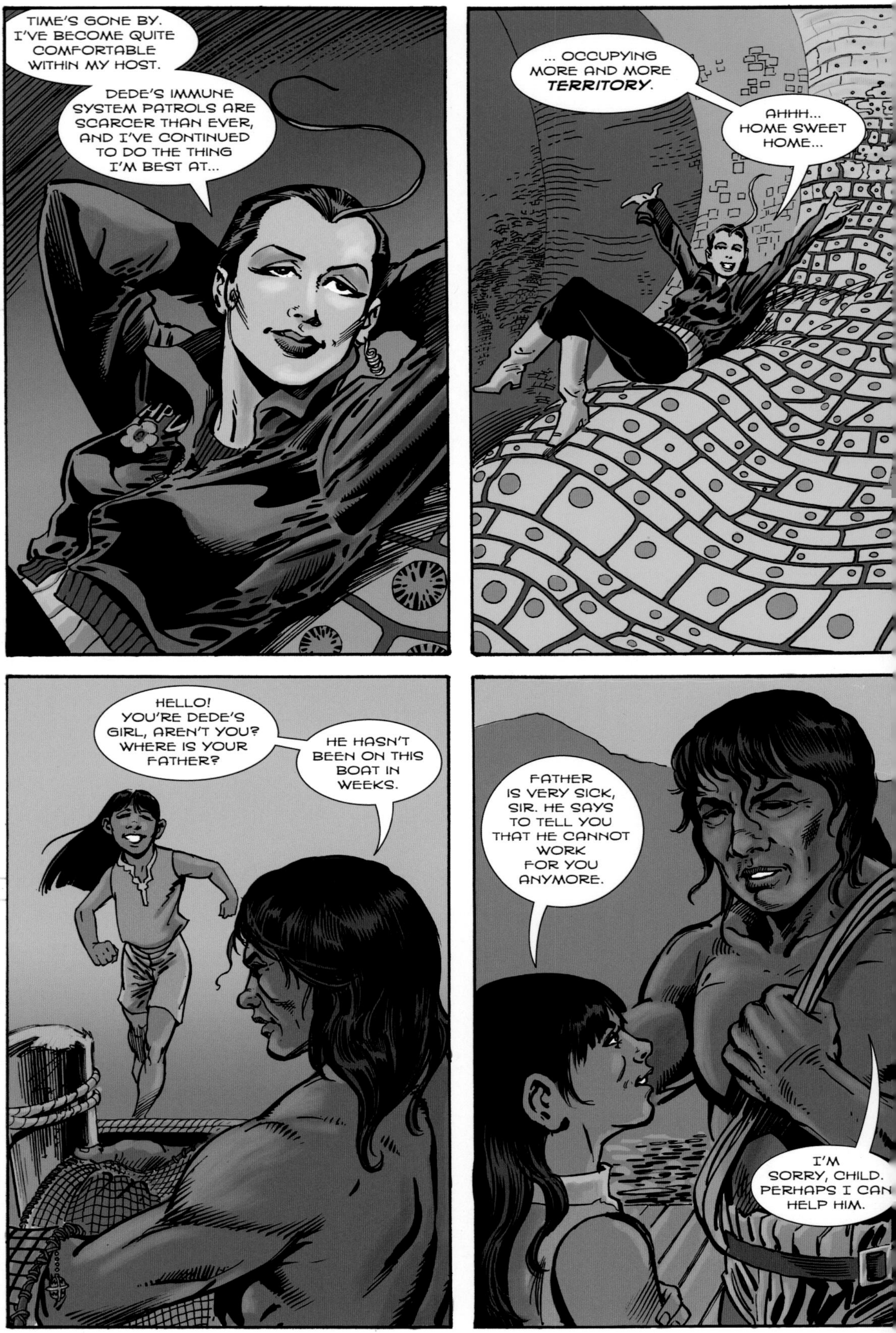
TIME'S GONE BY. I'VE BECOME QUITE COMFORTABLE WITHIN MY HOST.
DEDE'S IMMUNE SYSTEM PATROLS ARE SCARCER THAN EVER, AND I'VE CONTINUED TO DO THE THING I'M BEST AT...
... OCCUPYING MORE AND MORE *TERRITORY*.
AHHH... HOME SWEET HOME...
HELLO! YOU'RE DEDE'S GIRL, AREN'T YOU? WHERE IS YOUR FATHER?
HE HASN'T BEEN ON THIS BOAT IN WEEKS.
FATHER IS VERY SICK, SIR. HE SAYS TO TELL YOU THAT HE CANNOT WORK FOR YOU ANYMORE.
I'M SORRY, CHILD. PERHAPS I CAN HELP HIM.

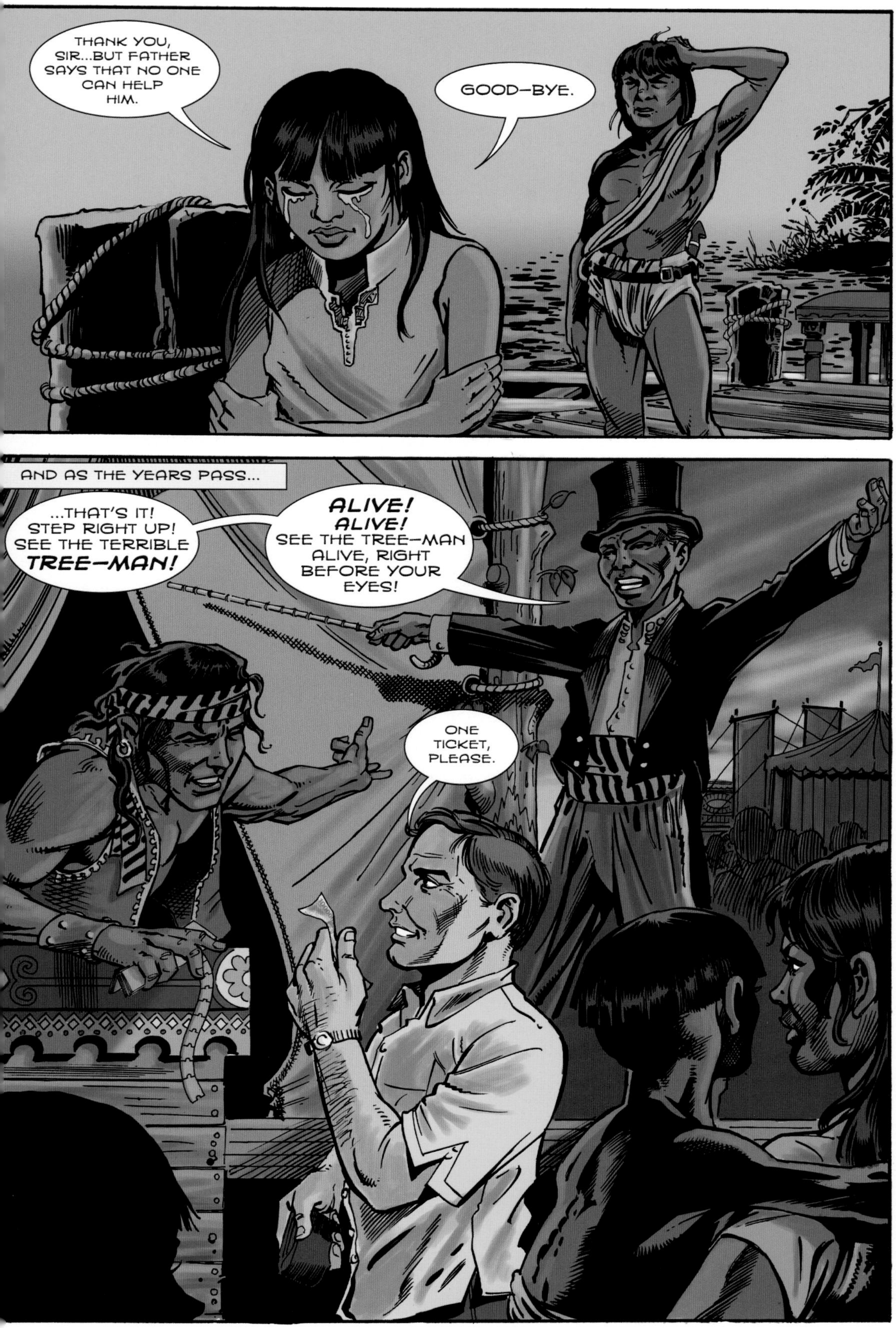
THANK YOU, SIR...BUT FATHER SAYS THAT NO ONE CAN HELP HIM.
GOOD-BYE.
AND AS THE YEARS PASS...
...THAT'S IT! STEP RIGHT UP! SEE THE TERRIBLE TREE-MAN!
ALIVE! ALIVE! SEE THE TREE-MAN ALIVE, RIGHT BEFORE YOUR EYES!
ONE TICKET, PLEASE.

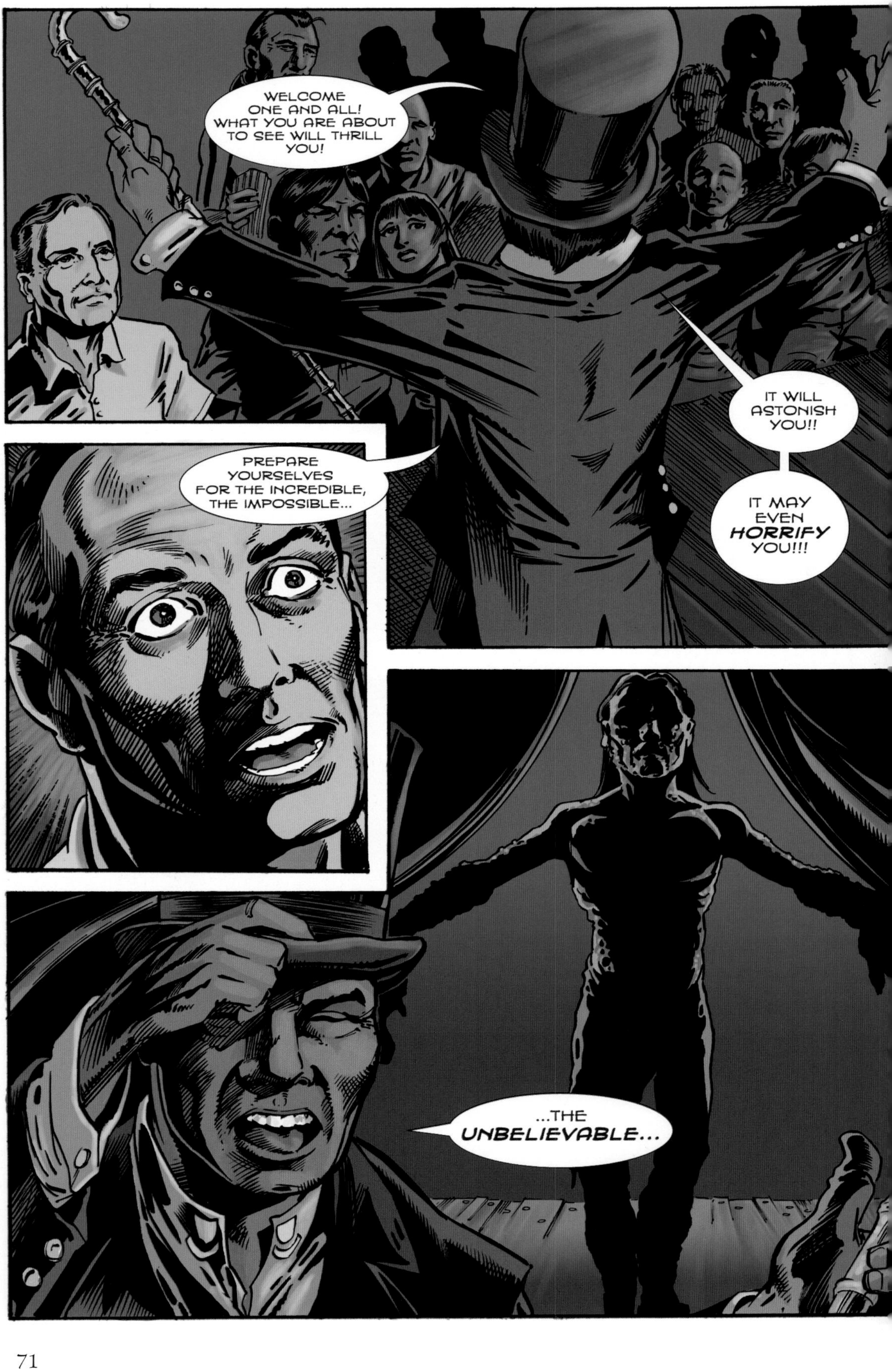
WELCOME ONE AND ALL! WHAT YOU ARE ABOUT TO SEE WILL THRILL YOU!
IT WILL ASTONISH YOU!!
IT MAY EVEN *HORRIFY* YOU!!!
PREPARE YOURSELVES FOR THE INCREDIBLE, THE IMPOSSIBLE...
...THE *UNBELIEVABLE*...

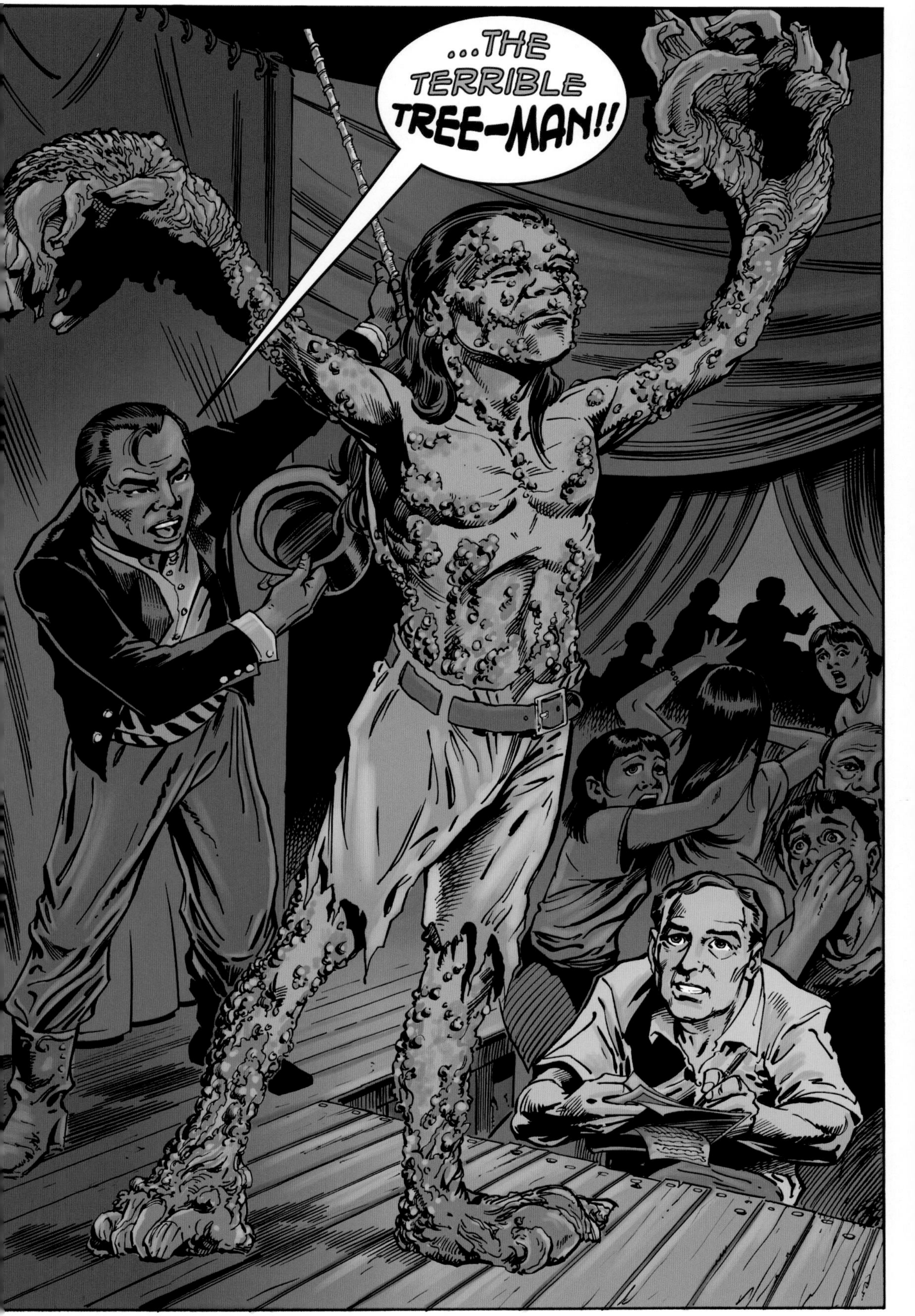
...THE TERRIBLE TREE-MAN!!

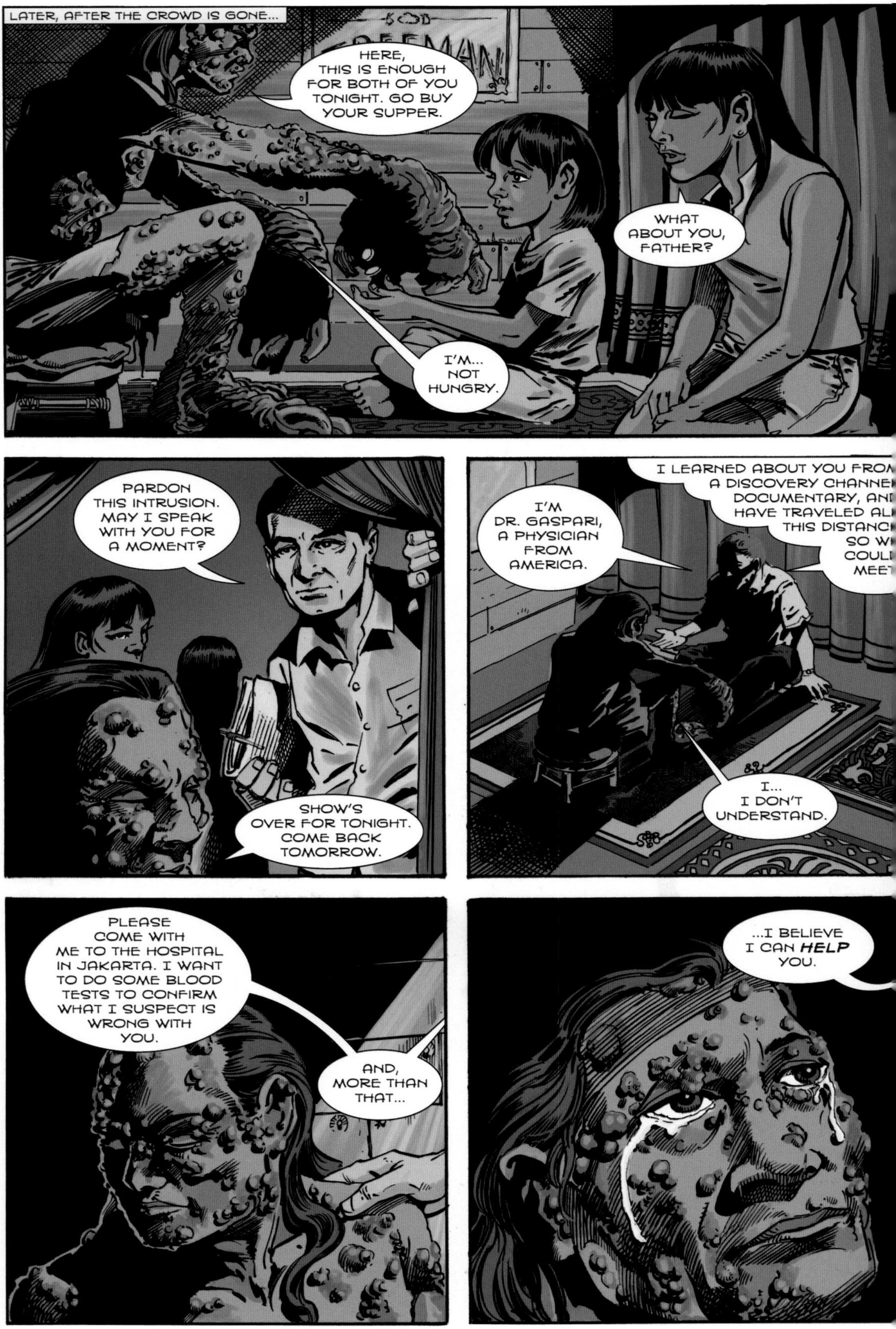
LATER, AFTER THE CROWD IS GONE...
HERE, THIS IS ENOUGH FOR BOTH OF YOU TONIGHT. GO BUY YOUR SUPPER.
WHAT ABOUT YOU, FATHER?
I'M... NOT HUNGRY.
PARDON THIS INTRUSION. MAY I SPEAK WITH YOU FOR A MOMENT?
SHOW'S OVER FOR TONIGHT. COME BACK TOMORROW.
I'M DR. GASPARI, A PHYSICIAN FROM AMERICA.
I LEARNED ABOUT YOU FROM A DISCOVERY CHANNE DOCUMENTARY, AN HAVE TRAVELED AL THIS DISTANC SO W COUL MEET
I... I DON'T UNDERSTAND.
PLEASE COME WITH ME TO THE HOSPITAL IN JAKARTA. I WANT TO DO SOME BLOOD TESTS TO CONFIRM WHAT I SUSPECT IS WRONG WITH YOU.
AND, MORE THAN THAT...
...I BELIEVE I CAN *HELP* YOU.

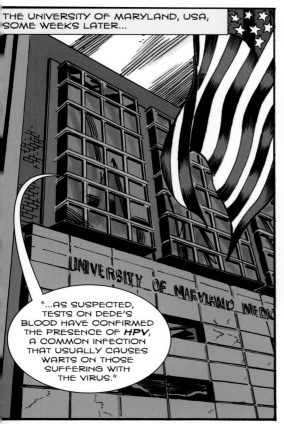

THE UNIVERSITY OF MARYLAND, USA, SOME WEEKS LATER...
"...AS SUSPECTED, TESTS ON DEDE'S BLOOD HAVE CONFIRMED THE PRESENCE OF **HPV**, A COMMON INFECTION THAT USUALLY CAUSES WARTS ON THOSE SUFFERING WITH THE VIRUS."
HOWEVER, THE MAIN CAUSE OF DEDE'S UNIQUE PROBLEM IS AN UNCOMMON **GENETIC FAULT** THAT IMPEDES HIS OWN NATURAL IMMUNITY, DENYING HIS BODY'S ABILITY TO CONTAIN THE DISEASED GROWTHS, ALLOWING THEM TO **GROW OUT OF CONTROL**.
USUALLY WE'D SUSPECT THE AIDS VIRUS IN SUCH A SUPPRESSED IMMUNE SYSTEM, BUT DEDE TESTED **NEGATIVE** FOR HIV.
ASIDE FROM THE WARTY TUMORS, DEDE HAS ENJOYED REMARKABLY GOOD HEALTH THROUGHOUT MOST OF HIS LIFE... WHICH WOULD NOT BE EXPECTED OF SOMEONE WITH SUCH A LOW COUNT OF CERTAIN KEY **WHITE BLOOD CELLS**.
I'D ESTIMATE THE LIKELIHOOD OF ANYONE HAVING THIS SAME IMMUNE DEFICIENCY AT LESS THAN ONE IN A MILLION.
WE HAVE SOMETHING HERE THAT IS VERY **RARE...**

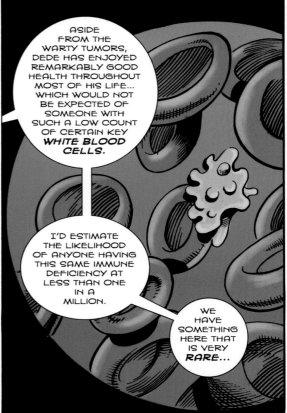

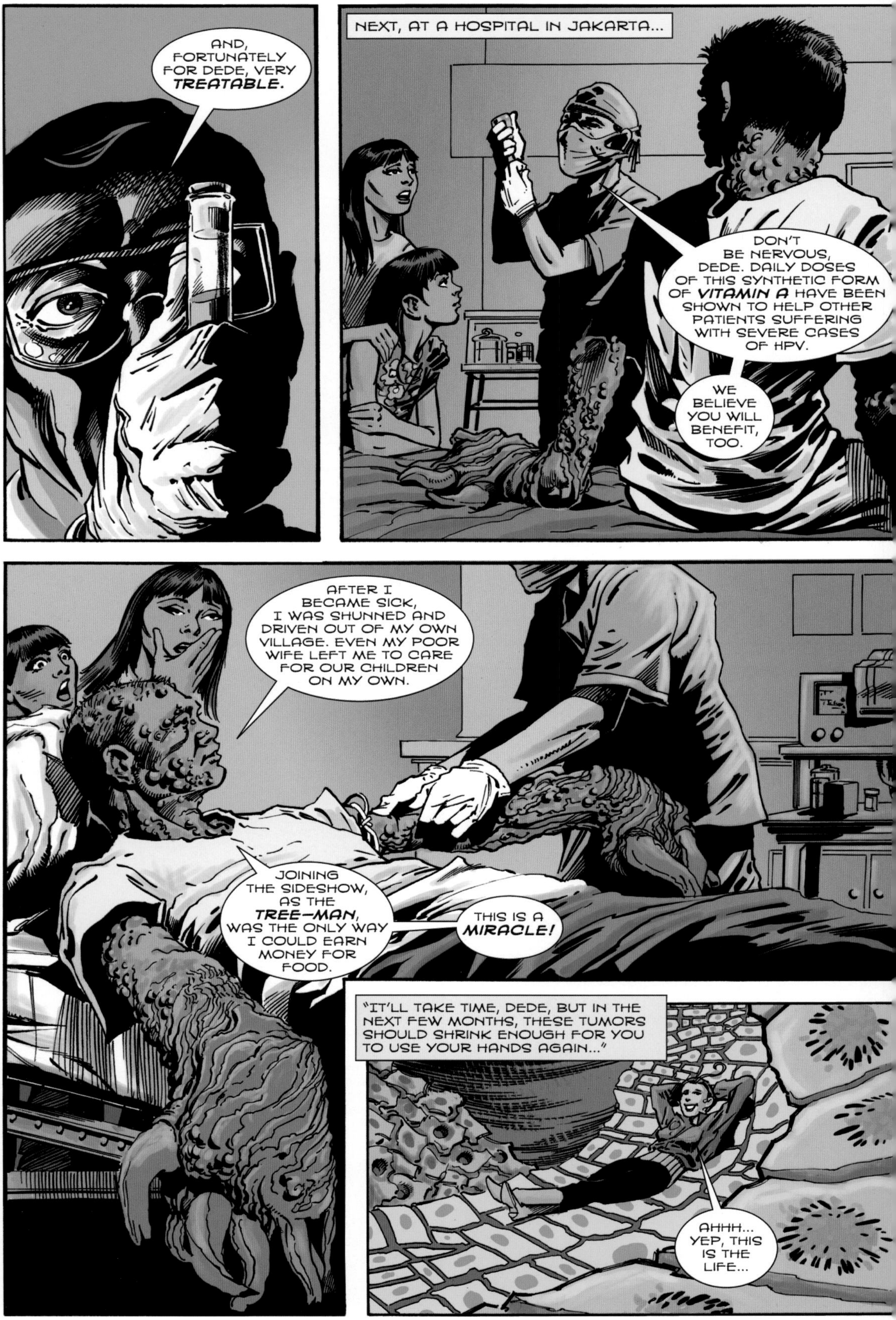
AND, FORTUNATELY FOR DEDE, VERY TREATABLE.
NEXT, AT A HOSPITAL IN JAKARTA...
DON'T BE NERVOUS, DEDE. DAILY DOSES OF THIS SYNTHETIC FORM OF VITAMIN A HAVE BEEN SHOWN TO HELP OTHER PATIENTS SUFFERING WITH SEVERE CASES OF HPV.
WE BELIEVE YOU WILL BENEFIT, TOO.
AFTER I BECAME SICK, I WAS SHUNNED AND DRIVEN OUT OF MY OWN VILLAGE. EVEN MY POOR WIFE LEFT ME TO CARE FOR OUR CHILDREN ON MY OWN.
JOINING THE SIDESHOW, AS THE TREE-MAN, WAS THE ONLY WAY I COULD EARN MONEY FOR FOOD.
THIS IS A MIRACLE!
"IT'LL TAKE TIME, DEDE, BUT IN THE NEXT FEW MONTHS, THESE TUMORS SHOULD SHRINK ENOUGH FOR YOU TO USE YOUR HANDS AGAIN..."
AHHH... YEP, THIS IS THE LIFE...

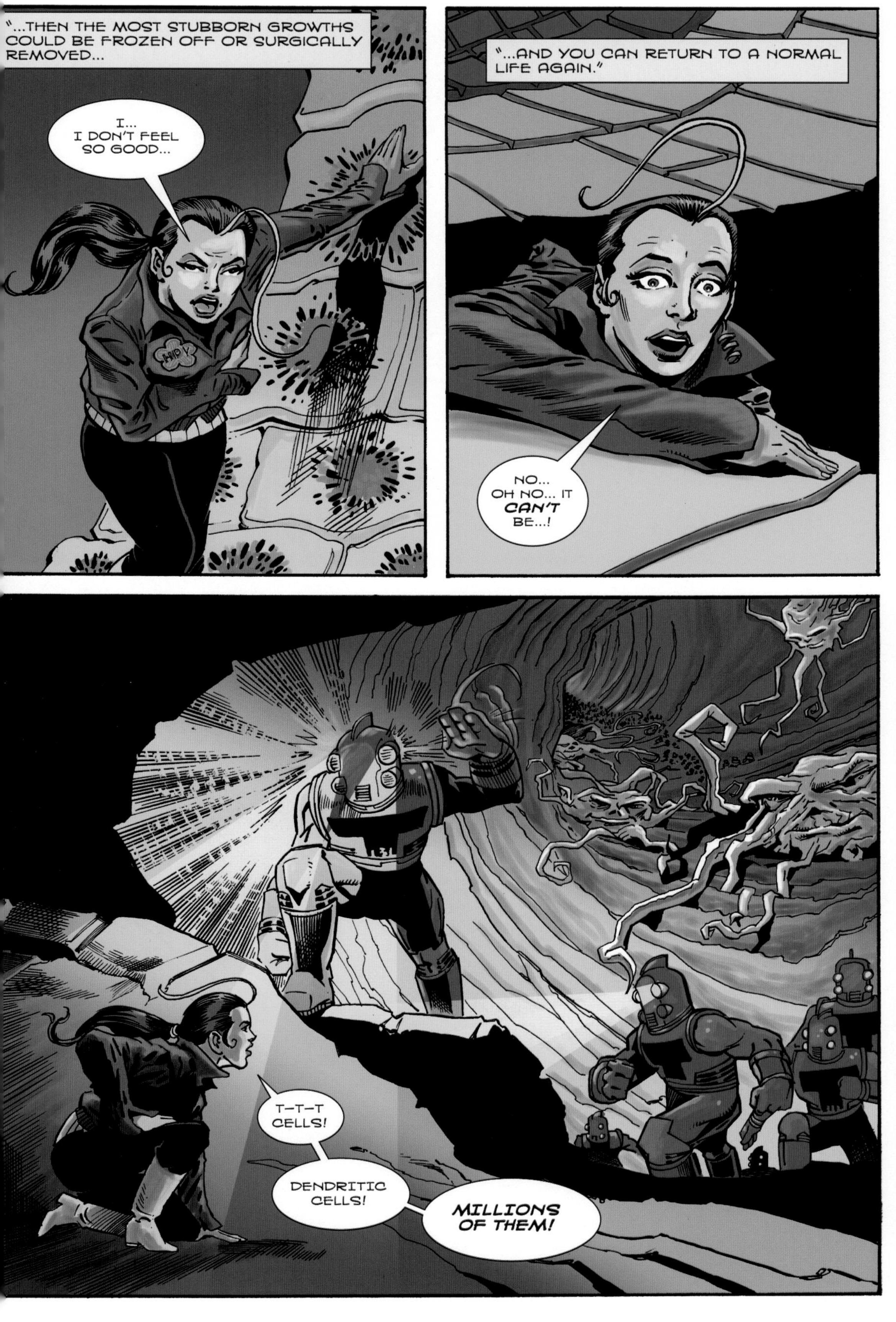
"...THEN THE MOST STUBBORN GROWTHS COULD BE FROZEN OFF OR SURGICALLY REMOVED...
I... I DON'T FEEL SO GOOD...
"...AND YOU CAN RETURN TO A NORMAL LIFE AGAIN."
NO... OH NO... IT *CAN'T* BE...!
T-T-T CELLS!
DENDRITIC CELLS!
MILLIONS OF THEM!

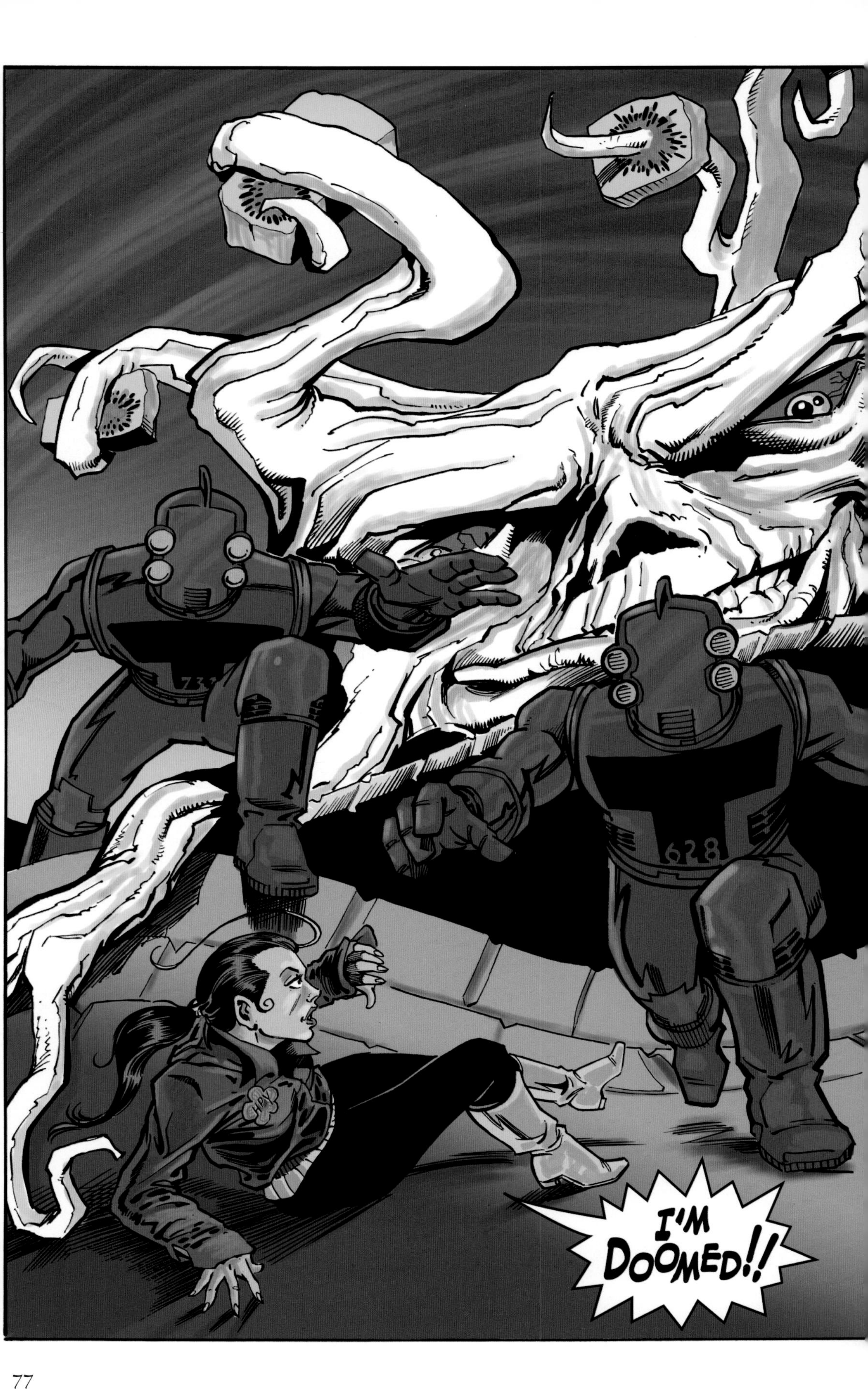
733
628
I'M DOOMED!!

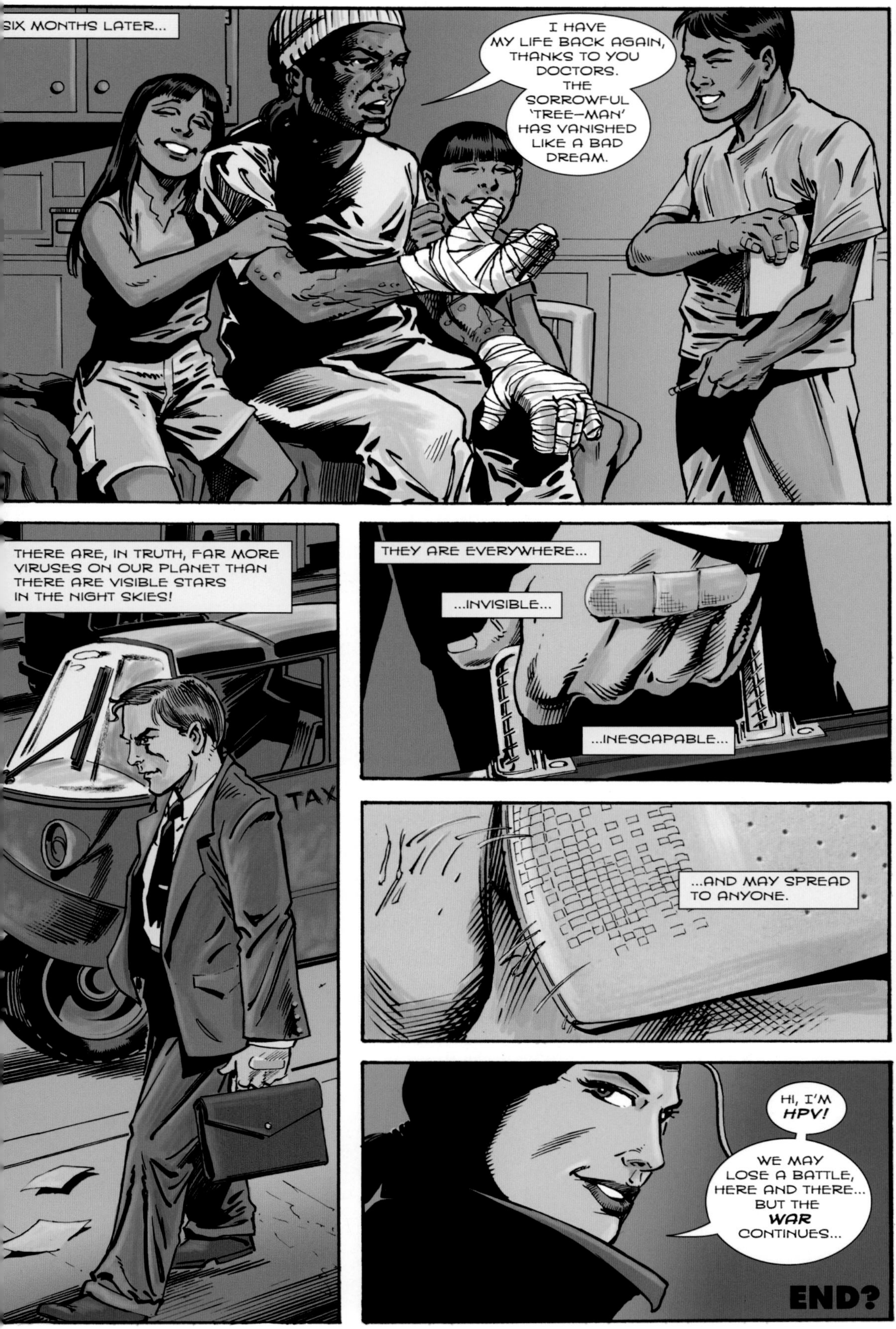
SIX MONTHS LATER...
I HAVE MY LIFE BACK AGAIN, THANKS TO YOU DOCTORS. THE SORROWFUL 'TREE-MAN' HAS VANISHED LIKE A BAD DREAM.
THERE ARE, IN TRUTH, FAR MORE VIRUSES ON OUR PLANET THAN THERE ARE VISIBLE STARS IN THE NIGHT SKIES!
THEY ARE EVERYWHERE...
...INVISIBLE...
...INESCAPABLE...
...AND MAY SPREAD TO ANYONE.
HI, I'M *HPV!*
WE MAY LOSE A BATTLE, HERE AND THERE... BUT THE *WAR* CONTINUES...
END?

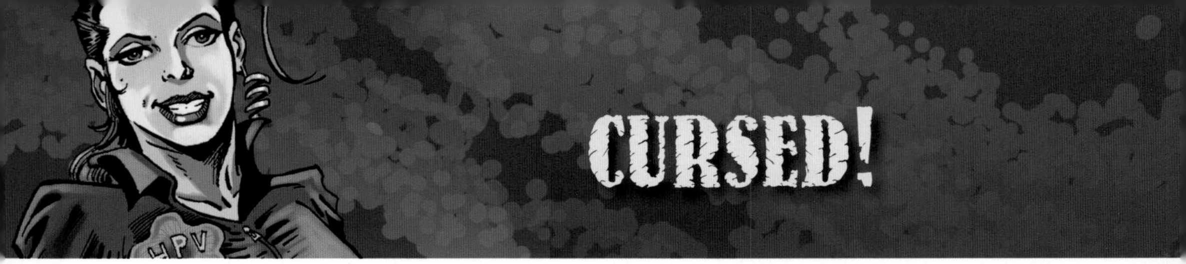
HPV

CURSED!

by Ann Downer-Hazell

Can a virus turn a man into a tree? Maybe not, but one virus turned a man in Indonesia into a "tree-man". That virus is the Human Papillomavirus, or HPV.

Like other viruses, HPV can enter its human through even the tiniest cut. Once inside, the virus takes over the cell to make copies of its own genetic code. It can also override the cell's natural defenses, prompting it to divide out of control.

Your immune system's first line of defense against an HPV invasion are special cells called dendritic cells. Dendritic cells send out patrols of T cells, your immune system's first responders. But since HPV is small and the "territory" that T cells have to patrol is large, HPV can hide from your immune system's defenses and escape detection. HPV has also found ways to short-circuit the cell's natural alarm system that normally brings T cells to the rescue, tricking the cell into thinking that all's well.

HPV can lie dormant in its host's cells for years, the only symptoms a few small warts. But without diagnosis and treatment HPV spreads throughout the body, further shutting down the immune system and infecting more and more cells.

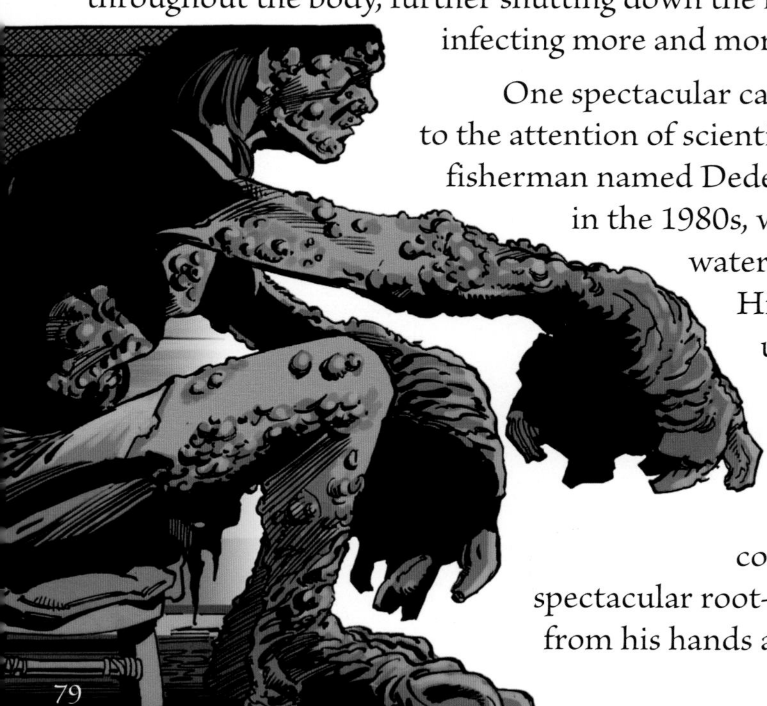

One spectacular case of HPV infection came to the attention of scientists in 2007. An Indonesian fisherman named Dede was infected as a teenager in the 1980s, when contaminated river water entered a cut in his knee. His HPV infection went undiagnosed and untreated for decades, and a few warts on his leg grew and grew until Dede was almost completely covered with warts, including spectacular root-like growths extending from his hands and feet. Unable to work, shunned by his neighbors, and abandoned by his wife, Dede was reduced to exhibiting himself in a carnival sideshow as the "tree-man" to earn enough money to support his children. Then Anthony Gaspari, M.D., a dermatologist with the University of Maryland, heard of Dede's plight through a TV documentary on the Discovery Channel. Suspecting a virus might be responsible for Dede's condition, Gaspari traveled to Indonesia to examine him.

Tests of the "tree-man's" blood showed he had an unusually low white blood cell count, a sign of a malfunctioning immune system. This led Gaspari to suspect that he might have HIV, the virus that causes AIDS. But Dede tested negative for HIV. In fact, apart from his disfiguring warts, he enjoyed remarkably good health.

Gaspari conducted new blood tests and the results confirmed his suspicion that Dede was infected with human papillomavirus. But HPV didn't usually cause such extreme warts. Why had the tree-man's skin cells gone haywire? Further tests revealed that a rare genetic mutation had left Dede's immune system unable to fight the virus and allowed it to multiply unchecked. The "typo" in Dede's DNA was incredibly rare; Gaspari estimated the chances of such a mutation were one in a million.

Gaspari had hopes that Dede's infection could be reversed, even though it had gone untreated for decades. He started his patient on daily doses of synthetic Vitamin A, which had been used successfully to treat other cases of extreme HPV infection, and drugs to boost his immune system. These drugs should have allowed Dede's T cells to recognize and fight HPV, but the treatment proved toxic. Surgeons removed most of Dede's warts, but without a way to reverse the genetic fault that had given HPV its foothold, the warts began to grow back. Soon after Dede's initial treatment in 2008, the tree-like growths on his hands and feet began to return.

Doctors estimate it will take two surgeries a year for the rest of his life to keep the warts at bay and give Dede a better quality of life. Dede and his Indonesian medical team face an ongoing struggle to stay one step ahead of HPV.

Acknowledgments

We are grateful to Moira Rankin, President of Soundprint Media Center, Inc., for her collaboration, advice, and for the remarkable radio documentaries about viruses produced for the World of Viruses SEPA project.

Many scientists guided our work and reviewed its production. We especially acknowledge the enormous help of Anisa Kaenjak Angeletti and Peter Angeletti, Nebraska Center for Virology & School of Biological Sciences, UNL, who reviewed each stage of the comics and essays. Individual comics were inspired and reviewed by the following scientists: James Van Etten and David Dunigan, Department of Plant Pathology, UNL; Fernando Osorio, Gustavo Delhon, and David R. Smith, School of Veterinary Medicine and Biomedical Sciences, UNL; Levon Abrahamyan, Nebraska Center for Virology, UNL; and Willie Wilson, Bigelow Laboratory for Ocean Sciences.

For many kinds of assistance and advice, we thank Amy Spiegel, Center for Instructional Innovation, UNL; Kristin Watkins, Center for Preparedness Education, University of Nebraska Medical Center & Creighton University Medical Center; Ian Cottingham and Kevin Farrell, Department of Computer Science and Engineering, UNL; Adam Wagler, College of Journalism & Mass Communications, UNL; Camillia Matuk, David Uttal, and Benjamin Jee, Multidisciplinary Program in Education Sciences, Northwestern University; Leah Carpenter, School of Public Health at the University of Nebraska Medical Center; Julia McQuillan and the staff of the Bureau of Sociological Research, UNL; Nathan Meier and Joel Brehm, Office of Research, UNL; Cindy Loope, University of Nebraska State Museum; NET, Nebraska Educational Telecommunications; Bruce Erickson, Science Museum of Minnesota; and, finally, our enthusiastic and tireless NIH program officer, L. Tony Beck.

Image Credits

Influenza virus illustrated by Dan Higgins and provided by Douglas Jordan, Centers for Disease Control and Prevention (CDC). Visit http://phil.cdc.gov/phil/.

Foot and mouth disease (FMD) virus image by Jean-Yves Sgro, Ph.D., University of Wisconsin-Madison, USA. Copyright Jean-Yves Sgro/Visuals Unlimited. Software used to create FMD virus image: VMD - Visual Molecular Dynamics. Visit http://www.ks.uiuc.edu/Research/vmd/.

Emiliania huxleyi algal image was inspired by SEMs produced by Dr. Jeremy Young, The Natural History Museum, London.

Comic fonts by Blambot.com

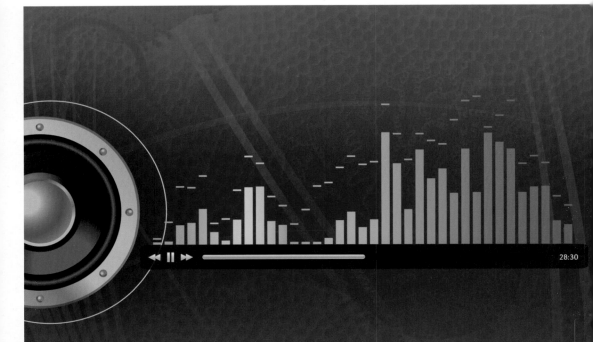

28:30

SOUNDPRINT
MEDIA CENTER, INC.

Real-life science behind the
comics – hear the stories of
survivors, researchers and
scientists who overcome obstacles
to solve the mysteries of the
World of Viruses.

Listen to radio documentaries.

http://soundprint.org/worldofvirus/